NEPAL'S MAOIST MOVEMENT AND IMPLICATIONS FOR INDIA AND CHINA

The Regional Centre for Strategic Studies (RCSS) is an independent, non-profit and non-governmental organization for collaborative research, networking and interaction on strategic and international issues pertaining to South Asia. Set up in 1992, the RCSS is based in Colombo, Sri Lanka.

The RCSS is a South Asian forum for studies, training and multi-track dialogue and deliberation on issues of regional interest. All activities of RCSS are designed with a South Asia focus and are usually participated by experts from all South Asian countries. The Centre is envisaged as a forum for advancing the cause of cooperation, security, conflict resolution, confidence building, peace and development in the countries of the South Asian region.

The RCSS serves its South Asian and international constituency by: (a) networking programmes that promote interaction, communication and exchange between institutions and individuals within and outside the region engaged in South Asian strategic studies; (b) organizing regional workshops and seminars and sponsoring and coordinating collaborative research; and (c) disseminating output of the research through publications which include books, monographs and a quarterly newsletter. The RCSS facilitates scholars and other professionals of South Asia to address, mutually and collectively, problems and issues of topical interest for all countries of the region.

Queries may be addressed to:

Regional Centre for Strategic Studies
2 Elibank Road
Colombo 5
SRI LANKA
Tel: (94-11) 2599734, 2599735
Fax: 2599993; e-mail: rcss@sri.lanka.net
RCSS website: http://www.rcss.org

RCSS Policy Studies 27

Nepal's Maoist Movement and Implications for India and China

NISHCHAL NATH PANDEY

REGIONAL CENTRE FOR STRATEGIC STUDIES
COLOMBO

MANOHAR
2005

Published by
Ajay Kumar Jain *for*
Manohar Publishers & Distributors
4753/23 Ansari Road, Daryaganj
New Delhi 110 002
and
Regional Centre for Strategic Studies
2 Elibank Road
Colombo 5
SRI LANKA
Tel: (94-11) 2599734-5; Fax: 2599993;
e-mail: rcss@sri.lanka.net
Website: http://www.rcss.org

First published April 2005
Reprinted August 2005

ISBN 81-7304-623-9

Typeset by
Kohli Print
Delhi 110 051

Printed at
Lordson Publishers Pvt. Ltd.
Delhi 110 007

Distributed in South Asia by
FOUNDATION
BOOKS
4381/4, Ansari Rorad
Daryaganj, New Delhi 110 002
and its branches at Mumbai, Hyderabad,
Bangalore, Chennai, Kolkata

Contents

RCSS is grateful to the
Ford Foundation for its generous
support for the Kodikara Award
on which this report is based.

Acknowledgements

Who would have thought that when the Maoist rebellion started in 1996, in a matter of just five years it would turn out to become a never ending nightmare for the state and hold the entire state's economy and polity to ransom? As Kathmandu revelled in the pleasures of the newly won democratic freedom (which for many was the liberty to plunder the state treasury), the other side was earnestly setting up its propaganda, ideological, and training wings in concert with its armed units for a 'decisive struggle of the proletariat against the feudal, capitalist bourgeoisie to establish a dictatorship of the oppressed class'. It seemed that the country was heading on an unmarked road to an unknown destination.

Although a lot has been written on the Maoist movement of Nepal, most of it comprises newspaper articles or news reports. But even so, a systematic record of daily events is not available *for the common man* to read and evaluate. Similarly, there is also a need for more coherent and analytical publications to read and evaluate the situation on the ground. That being so, I have ventured to put forward a overview of the movement, with briefs on the history of Nepal's extreme left groups, the genesis of the crisis, its growing influence, and, ultimately, the likely impact that it is going to have on India and China, Nepal's two neighbours that are, according to international security watchers, 'the military and economic heavyweights of the twenty-first century'.

I am grateful to the Regional Centre for Strategic Studies (RCSS), Colombo, and the support and encouragement of its former Executive Director, Maj. Gen. Dipankar Banerjee (retd.), for granting me the prestigious Kodikara Award, with the help of which I was able to study this issue in detail. I am thankful to my supervisor, Prof. Krishna P. Khanal of Tribhuvan University, Kathmandu, for painstakingly going through the draft of this volume several times and advising me to pull up and put right several points that I had overlooked. I would like to thank the Executive Director of the RCSS, Prof. Sridhar K. Khatri, for publishing this work.

My sincere thanks go to the many officials, academics, and the common villagers whom I interacted with during the course of this study, particularly to those Nepalese whom I met in the Indian cities of Raxaul, Gorakhpur, and Delhi, whose moving and often distressing accounts were the experience of a lifetime.

The research methodology for this study is of my own choosing—simple interviews, personal exchanges, and detailed examinations of the events and developments. Needless to say, the views expressed here are my own, and do not reflect in any way the position of the organizations that I worked for or have been or am associated with.

I do not claim that the study is complete, but I am hopeful that anybody who reads this will have a clearer picture of the events taking place in Nepal, and of all the aspects of the insurgency and counter-insurgency operations that are going on. Even if the reader is left a little wiser on certain features of the Maoist movement upon reading this book, I will suppose that I have contributed at least a bit to a better understanding of the problem.

NISHCHAL NATH PANDEY

Introduction

Today Nepal is facing a crisis that is undermining the political, economic, social, and cultural base of its 'Nepali nationality'. In the five decades of its experiments with democracy, the country's political development has witnessed virtually all varieties of extremism, but it was with the launching of the Maoist movement that a vicious cycle of violence and counter-violence emerged from political instability, failed development, personal ambitions, and ineffective state response.

From a modest beginning in 1996 in a relatively small, isolated corner of the mid-hills, the Maoist movement has now come to engulf most parts of the hitherto peaceful kingdom and presented new challenges to the ethnic, religious, and cultural rubric of the country. It has caused enormous loss of human life and destruction of developmental infrastructure. The stated objectives of the 'People's War' of the CPN(Maoists) are to overthrow the bureaucratic-capitalist class and the monarchy, and force out hegemonic and imperialist forces from the country in order to establish a new democratic-socialist society. However, even with thousands killed, maimed and displaced, with billions of rupees having been spent to defeat the state or suppress the insurgents, and governments dismissed on not being able to restore normalcy, the insurgency goes on unabated, neither succeeding in overwhelming the state, nor conceding its demands.

The present study gives an overview of the roots of Marxist ideology in Nepal since the era of the Cold War and the achievements of the Maoists in China and the Naxalite movement in India. The steady advance of the armed movement in the last eight years, analysis of the costs and consequences of the ongoing catastrophe, the lost opportunities, and the dreams and hopes nurtured by those who died, both on the side of the government and of the Maoists are also discussed, with emphasis on the human dimension of the problem. The agony of the naive Nepali child turned into a child soldier, the torment of the harmless disabled, the elderly and the women caught between the two warring sides is more horrifying than what international NGOs, Kathmandu's cocktail-circuit elite, or this concise monograph can possibly portray.

Chapter 1 of the monograph provides a historical background to the communist movement of Nepal. Chapter 2 goes on to discuss the launching of the Maoist movement in 1996, and the causes behind its dramatic growth are discussed in Chapter 3. These initial chapters assess the performance of elected governments, their legitimacy to govern, and the necessity of corruption-free good governance as well as the importance of an effective law and order machinery in order to study the growth of the conflict. The objective of this is to highlight that, despite the wave of economic liberalization and privatization initiated in the early 1990s, the worsening economic conditions, low income of the general populace, and the perceived futility of the common man at his inability to participate in political decision-making processes have contributed to a great extent to what is today a pitched battle between the army and the Maoists. The Nepalese fought several wars against the Tibetans and the British, but today they are engaged in internecine warfare in dismal if spectacular fashion, negating its one-time image of a 'zone of peace'. The progress of the rebellion from a defensive, tactical stalemate to strategic offence is detailed in Chapter 4, and the government's attempts to defeat the insurgency by spending more than 25 per cent of its total revenue on security is looked at in Chapter 5. The implications of political instability and of international events like 11 September influencing the rebellion are covered in Chapter 6, which, perhaps for the first time, aroused American interest in Nepal directly.

Whereas the killing of non-combatants, bomb blasts, extortion and calling for Nepal *bandhs* and strikes of industrial and educational institutions are characteristic of the human rights abuses on the part of the rebels, the state response in the form of disappearances and extrajudicial killings has degenerated into human rights violations, which have been studied in Chapter 7. Therefore, while it is contended that this insurgency, more than any other in the region, has to be fought as much with rural development, economic revival, and effective governance as with military might, it has also highlighted the pernicious influences that the Nepali polity, caste hierarchy, and bureaucratic sluggishness can pose to a determined and resolute approach to eliminating the roots of the problem. Chapter 8 gives an overview of the failed negotiations, and discusses the future prospects while focusing on the urgency for both sides to come together without inflicting any further loss to a poor nation.

Whenever a ceasefire is announced between the government and the rebels, it raises the expectations of the common man, and at least brings a pause to the almost continuous killings. Importantly, the principal state actors have to be trained in the intricacy and skills required for peaceful negotiations, as experiments without proper homework and orientation can prove to be counter-productive, if not disastrous.

Due to Nepal's unique history and geo-strategic location, particular emphasis on the implications for India and China of this ongoing conflict in the short and the longer term have been examined in Chapters 9 and 10. These economic and military giants of the twenty-first century well realize that continuing instability in Nepal can be a headache for both if Nepal cannot resolve its problems on its own, and plunges into political and social chaos and economic ruin. It will have political, security, social, and demographic consequences on, immediately, the bordering regions of these two neighbours, and subsequently on the hinterland. Both India and China currently have 7 per cent economic growth per annum and would not want their attention and energies to be diverted by destabilizing events in Nepal. Therefore, their stakes are high, next only to those of the hapless Nepalese. The study concludes with a general future outlook of the movement in the concluding Chapter 11.

Will the three power centres of the country—the monarchy, the political parties, and the Maoists—come together for the larger cause of unity and integrity of their nation, which was never colonized in its entire history, or will they continue jockeying with one another in frantic attempts at short-term gains to serve their vested interests? Given that the ultimate solution of the problem lies in a capable, visionary, and firm leadership and statesmanship, will the country be able to achieve this in the foreseeable future? If handled constructively, conflicts do open up possibilities for political and social transformation and economic progress. But, as Nepal stands at the crossroads between a stable and better future and the possibility of the country plunging deeper into a protracted conflict with all-round collateral effects, this is the question this monograph seeks to answer.

CHAPTER 1

History of Nepal's Communist Movement

The history of Nepal's left movement is a chequered one prone to splits and continuous divisions, uneven and, even, blurred in its policies and programmes. Due to inner-party rivalry and power play among individuals as well as disagreement on the viewing of contemporaneous political situation and methods of forging the movement forward, divisions have been frequent. After the establishment of democracy in the country in 1951, as a mixture of diverse governments and even political systems were introduced and began to fall apart, left parties with the new ideological appeal of Marxism and Leninism embarked on a journey that proved to be long and arduous. It must be emphasized here that both socialism and Marxism have been important elements of Nepalese intellectual life:

> [The] light of education and the canon of the Marxist ideology seemed to have entered Nepal almost the same time. Both Marxist and socialist ideologies appealed to the demands in Nepalese society for equality. Equality itself was not a new concept, but the possibility of its application to society as a whole was an intoxicating—even an explosive—political idea for people living in a society still in the shadow of caste hierarchy and feudal structures.[1]

INFLUENCE OF INDIAN STRUGGLE FOR INDEPENDENCE

Although the country had been totally closed to information and knowledge about the developments taking place in the outside world, deliberately curtailed by the repressive Rana regime which

[1] Martin Hoftun, William Raeper and John Whelpton, *People, Politics and Ideology: Democracy and Social Change in Nepal*, Kathmandu: Mandala Book Point, p. 234.

feared that the younger Nepalese generation would be persuaded by its influence, a sizeable number had received education in India and had a better awareness of the slowly but steadily crumbling British empire and the evolution of the worldwide communist movement. Furthermore, inspiration from Indian political developments has long been a hallmark of Nepalese political history. Nepalese students were especially motivated by the end of the British rule in India and with establishment of a Constituent Assembly that would ultimately frame the Indian Constitution, and set up a representative form of government. Both the major political parties, the Nepali Congress (under the name of the Nepal Prajatantra Congress) and the Communist Party of Nepal (CPN) were established in India. The latter was formally set up on 15 September 1949, and Man Mohan Adhikari became its first prime minister (referring to the post of general secretary) after being elected by the party's first congress held on 30 January 1954.[2] Among the members of its central committee was Ayodhaya Singh, who was a representative of the Communist Party of India (CPI).

The basic objectives as outlined in the policy and programmes of the party were to bestow sovereignty on the Nepalese people, and to elect an executive from a parliament duly elected by the people. With the call 'Hills, Peaks, Rivers, and Land for all, let us share. Why do we accept slavery?' it struggled to awaken the Nepalese populace. The Declaration also pointed out the direction of the Nepalese revolution against feudalism and imperialism in order to create a People's Democratic Nepal. Its pronouncement was simple and clear: 'CPN is dedicated to activate, organize and lead the emerging struggle of the working people towards victory. No terrorism and alluring propaganda can make it deviate from the track.'

Some time before 24 October 1950, as the New China News Agency news dispatch from Peking reported that the 'Chinese army had been ordered to free three million Tibetans from imperialist oppression and to consolidate the national defences of

[2] Grishma Bahadur Devkota, *Nepal ko Rajnitik Darpan* (Nepali, 'Nepal's Political Mirror'), Varanasi: Jaya Bharat Press, 1979, p. 35.

China's western corner', the Government of India (GOI) was already deeply anxious about the spread of communism right into the Himalayas, which they considered the defence wall of India. Nehru desired to help establish a stable political system in Nepal capable of withstanding any political challenge that might sooner or later come across the northern border. The rise of communism in Nepal was not impossible, as over a hundred years of Rana misrule with its limited social base had made the country's soil fertile for its growth. The people were primarily peasants, they were poor and had been oppressed by few feudal landlords, hereditary Rana rulers and the local administrators who behaved as extensions of the oligarchy. The threat wasn't imaginary: to the dismay of Delhi, the very first pamphlet issued by the party declared, 'Chinese people became victorious under the leadership of the Chinese Communist Party and their revolution has come right at our doorstep. We must also follow the same course.'

As long as the British power was dominant in Tibet, India's northern border obviously remained tight and secure, as it remained a buffer zone between India and China. But with the rise of China's military might and its occupation of Tibet, the latter not only ceased to be a buffer, more so, Nepal's position as a frontier state *vis-à-vis* India's strategic concerns came to the fore. Therefore, if Nepal fell under the influence of China or any inimical power, the entire Indo-Gangetic plain would be gravely exposed, and whatever little meaning the Himalayan barrier had would be considerably reduced.[3] In a letter to Prime Minister Jawaharlal Nehru on 7 November 1950, Sardar Patel expressed similar fears, that with the disappearance of Tibet, the expansion of China had 'almost come up to our gates', and went on to alert him that 'instead of having to deal with isolated communist pockets in Telengana and Warangal we may have to deal with communist threats to our security along our northern and north-eastern frontiers where, for supplies of arms and ammunition, they can safely depend on communist arsenals in China'.

[3] Ramakant and M.D. Dharamdasani, 'India's Attitude Towards Nepal', in *International Relations and Foreign Policy of India: India's Neighbors and her Foreign Policy*, ed. V. Grover, New Delhi: Deep and Deep Publications, 1992, p. 214.

Yet, the Rana government itself seemed to view the rise of communist power in China more as an excuse for retaining its political system intact rather than liberalizing its rigid style of functioning. In speeches made during his state visit to India in February 1950, Mohan Shumsher defended the Rana system as a bulwark against communist subversion from the north.[4] But with the crumbling of Tibet, India finalized a Treaty of Peace and Friendship with the Rana regime in order to safeguard its frontier. Signed between Mohan Shumsher and India's Ambassador to Nepal, Chandreshwar Prasad Narain Singh, on 31 July 1950, the Treaty recognized the ancient ties which had existed between Nepal and India, and desired to further strengthen and develop those ties and perpetuate peace between the two countries.

It must be appreciated at this point that enlightened and politically aware Nepalese had welcomed the independence of India enthusiastically, with the hope that free India would directly and actively come to help them in their fight against the tyranny of the Ranas. However, they soon found that the Indian government was doing very little for their cause. Their arch enemy, Mohan Shumsher, and the Indian government signed treaties of friendship and trade. In other words, the GOI, in their opinion, was toeing the same old British line in Nepal. This is how the anti-Indian feeling in Nepal started.[5] In fact, the psychological impact of this move of forging a treaty with the last Rana prime minister by India has remained in the minds of the Nepalese even till today—that of compulsion when internally vulnerable, and abandonment when the interest had somehow been fulfilled.

INVOLVEMENT OF THE COMMUNIST PARTY

On the critical question of the actual contribution of the newly-formed CPN in the revolution of 1950–1 to oust the Rana regime, a number of contrasting arguments exist. While Comrade

[4] Bhuwan L. Joshi and Leo E. Rose, *Democratic Innovations in Nepal: A Case Study of Political Acculturation*, Berkeley: University of California Press, 1966, p. 70.

[5] Krishna P. Khanal, 'Anti-India Feeling in South Asia: A Case of Nepal', in Grover, op. cit., n. 3 above, pp. 230–1.

Pushpalal recalls the forming of several freedom-fighters' units during the struggle led by the Nepali Congress (NC) under the leadership of Matrika Prasad Koirala, Keshar Jung Rayamajhi, founder member of the CPN and currently the Chairman of the Raj Parishad Standing Committee, states, on the other hand, that the NC did not wish to collaborate with the CPN on the grounds that: (1) the party was newly-formed and did not possess a strong militant base, and (2) there was strong opposition from India against tying up with the CPN. 'Hence, our involvement in the "oust Rana movement" was primarily individual-oriented and not officially on behalf of the party.'[6] Whatever the case, the revolution was a surprise to the Ranas. It was a classic case of the king and the people coming together and unifying against the oppression and tyranny of over a century. In fact, the revolt can be said to have begun the same day King Tribhuvan, along with most members of his family, flew to Delhi in an aircraft of the Indian Air Force. He had previously taken asylum inside the Indian Embassy on 10 November 1950 to force the Ranas to yield: instead, they chose to crown four-year-old HRH Prince Gyanendra in his place. Upon hearing this news, the NC mobilized volunteers to strike Birgunj, a southern border town. They succeeded, and forged ahead to fight all along the other districts of the Nepal–India border, including Jhapa and Biratnagar. Among the places captured by the NC were Kailali, Kanchanpur, Narayanpur, Bhagavanpur, Bhojpur, etc. Probably the most embarrassing for the government were the developments in Kathmandu and within the Rana family. Massive demonstrations in the capital on 26 and 28 November 1950 demanded the restoration of King Tribhuvan and an end to Rana tyranny. The government had to resort to gunfire, and two demonstrators were killed.[7]

As street pressure was building up, Prime Minister Mohan Shumsher sent Gen. Vijaya Shumsher and Gen. Keshar Shumsher to negotiate first with the GOI, and then with King Tribhuvan and the NC leaders. In a memorandum submitted to the Mohan Shumsher government on 8 December 1950, the GOI stated:

[6] K.C. Surendra, *History of Communist Movement in Nepal*, vol. I, Kathmandu, 2000, p. 45.

[7] Joshi and Rose, op. cit., n. 4 above, p. 70.

The Government of India's primary objective is that Nepal should be independent, progressive and strong. For this purpose they regard immediate constitutional changes, which will satisfy popular opinion, and be acceptable to important nonofficial organizations of Nepalese nationals as urgent. They suggest the following measures: (1) that a Constituent Assembly composed entirely of properly elected members should be brought into being as soon as possible to draw up a Constitution for Nepal; (2) pending the meeting of the Constituent Assembly mentioned above an interim government, which will include persons representative of popular opinion and enjoying public confidence should be established. This body should also include members of the Rana family, one of whom should be Prime Minister. This body should act as a cabinet on the principle of joint responsibility and should frame its own rules of business; and (3) King Tribhuvan should continue as King in the interests of the realm.[8]

The emphasis of the letter on the election of a Constituent Assembly and the formation of an interim government prior to the election are an important case in point.

It was evident, by now, that the GOI was not siding with the Ranas. Its policy towards Nepal in general, and the Ranas in particular, was influenced heavily by the liberal ideology of the NC leaders who had themselves participated in the quit India movement, been imprisoned, and suffered the same hardships as the Indian leaders. Moreover, Matrika Prasad Koirala, Dr Dilli Raman Regmi, B.P. Koirala, etc., had developed personal relationships with top Indian leaders who were by this time at the helm of affairs. Therefore, although meticulous diplomatic stratagems required that extracting maximum leverage from an unstable Nepal was feasible, emotional attachment with the Nepali revolutionaries, coupled with the desire for stability *vis-à-vis* the growth of communism compelled India to side with the revolutionaries. India allowed a young socialist, Bhola Chatterjee, to visit Myanmar (then Burma) and pick up a plane load of arms from the socialist government in power there.

U Nu was the prime minister and Ne Win the army chief. The plane landed in Bihar, and the arms went to the Nepali Congress partisans across

[8] K.P. Karunakaran, *India in World Affairs 1950–3*, London: Oxford University Press, 1958, p. 194.

the border. On Nov. 10, 1950 the N.C., using these Burmese weapons (plus 400 guns from police arsenal in Bihar gifted by the state government), launched an armed struggle against the Rana government to establish democracy in Nepal.[9]

Although the government (through its embassy in Delhi) began issuing statements implying that the NC rebels were trained, encouraged, and equipped by a certain group of Indians, it had to succumb to the internal problem stemming from massive political rallies and armed struggle. Ultimately, upon completion of the negotiations conducted by Gen. Vijaya and Gen. Keshar in New Delhi, Prime Minister Mohan Shumsher finally gave up on 8 January. He promised elections, based on adult suffrage, to be held no later than 1952 in order to form a Constituent Assembly, which would then draw up a Constitution for the country. He also proclaimed that an interim government comprising 14 ministers would be established immediately.

THE SEED IS PLANTED

A good beginning on the path of democracy, freedom, and liberty should have paved the way for a stable political environment in the country. On the contrary, however, a sizeable number of radical mutineers denounced the Delhi Agreement, maintaining that 'the Nepali Congress leaders had given way to the petty interests of 'C' class Ranas that were wanting to take revenge with the 'A' class for dismissing them into forced exile a few years ago'. A group dissatisfied with the Delhi Agreement not only remained on the scene, but was even encouraged with the persuasion of Dr K.I. Singh, a senior NC leader, to continue with the armed struggle against the Ranas despite the signing of the Agreement and the formation of a coalition government.

The situation turned ugly on the night of 21 January 1952, as the Rakshya Dal staged a revolt, freed the imprisoned Dr Singh, and seized key government installations, including the radio and wireless stations in Kathmandu. No one knows for sure the actual involvement of the communists in this action, but Matrika Prasad

[9] M. J. Akbar, *Nehru: The Making of India*, London: Viking, 1988, p. 553.

Koirala decided to quell the mutiny by force, and subsequently banned the CPN.

As a blessing in disguise, the activities of the party did not stagnate with the government ban: instead, the ban resulted in advancing its charisma and aura, as often happens with other banned movements around the world. A special focus on establishing camaraderie with other communist parties around the world ensured its permanence and long-term sustainability. Right after the revolt of Dr K.I. Singh, the party chose to send Gauri Bhakta Pradhan, a member of its Gandaki Zone Committee, for guerrilla training to China. He remained in Peking for two years and ten months; however, his skills were never put to use by the party due to internal rivalry.[10]

INTERNATIONAL CAMARADERIE

The CPN was, likewise, invited to send its senior comrades for the celebrations on the occasion of the tenth anniversary of the establishment of the People's Republic of China in September 1959. General Secretary Keshar Jung Rayamajhi, Pushpalal and P.B. Malla left Kathmandu on 23 September 1959 to participate in the anniversary functions and were received at the Peking [Beijing] airport by Premier Chou En-lai himself. Rayamajhi also met Chairman Mao Tse-tung [Mao Zedong] during his month-long sojourn. The CPN also built up relations with other communist parties around the world, and participated in various party meets, notably taking place in Moscow.

The magnetic appeal of communism was widely sensed when, despite its banned status, the CPN figured well in the first local-level elections based on adult franchise for the Kathmandu municipality held on 2 September 1953. The party won six seats out of a total 18, and Janak Man became the first mayor of Kathmandu. He later rose up the ladder of success by joining the judicial service. As a judge of Kathmandu district court, he decided on the famous and unique legal tangle involving Sucha Singh, the

[10] Surendra, op. cit., n. 6 above, p. 80.

assassin of Pratap Singh Kairon, chief minister of Punjab. This lawsuit, even linking itself with the extradition treaty between India and Nepal, was resolved after Judge Janak Man convicted Singh of murder and ultimately extradited him to India.

BEGINNING OF DISAGREEMENTS AND SPLITS

Eventually, as the ban on the party was lifted on 16 April 1956 just ahead of King Mahendra's coronation, sharp differences already existed within the party regarding the monarchy and the communist revolution in Nepal. This divergence in opinion was only to become visibly more acute in the days and years ahead. The party did not perform well in the first parliamentary elections held in February and April of 1959, winning just four seats in a house of 109. What is noteworthy here is the election manifesto issued by the party ahead of the elections. It declared that if the party was to form the government, 'it would review the existing treaty between Britain and Nepal to recruit Nepalese soldiers and would also check American infiltration inside Nepal'. Hence, it was apparant from this first official document that Nepalese leftist parties were always against American influence in the country.

When a three-member delegation led by General Secretary Man Mohan Adhikari left for China to participate in the Eighth Congress of the Chinese Communist Party, Adhikari fell ill and had to remain in China for several months. By a trick of fate, the leadership fell into the hands of Keshar Jung Rayamajhi. The Second National Congress of the party was held openly in the Phohora Palace in Kathmandu in June 1957. It approved the resolution of 'continuing the struggle for a Constituent Assembly and a republic' proposed by Pushpalal, although the party's control was taken away by a to-be staunch royalist. Therefore, it is apparent that the issues of the struggle for a Constituent Assembly and a republic have remained alive for well over 40 years; even though, its impact has been fluctuating alongside the changing political situations inside the country. In fact, Mohan Bikram Singh can be recognized one such odd communist leader who has vehemently and continuously carried the torch for the need of a Constituent Assembly throughout his long political career, analysis of which shall be done in the subsequent pages.

THE COUP OF 1960 AND THE CPN

Events were unfolding very quickly; both regional and international determinants were in favour of fulfilling the interests of the superpowers and regional heavyweights rather than simply adhering to the almost amorphous concepts of freedom and democracy. At the UN General Assembly in late 1960, the Prime Minister of the Soviet Union and the General Secretary of the Communist Party, Nikita Khrushchev, thumped his shoes on the table over an irksome issue that was being hotly debated.[11] A member of the Nepalese delegation, Biswo Bandu Thapa, chief whip of the ruling NC, attacked Khrushchev verbally and charged him of 'showing an un-parliamentary behavior in an international forum such as the United Nations'. In the midst of the entire international community, Khrushchev questioned the Nepali delegate whether Nepal 'had a parliament at [*sic*] the first place'. Thapa, a political heavyweight himself, promptly replied that 'not only did Nepal enjoy a parliamentary democracy but moreover a parliamentary delegation was visiting the Soviet Union the very same day at the invitation of the Supreme Soviet'. Fuming, the former responded that he would 'go back to Moscow and consult political geography to find out whether there was a parliament in Nepal'.

It is an irony of history that, by the time Khrushchev returned to Moscow, there indeed was no parliamentary democracy in Nepal. Whilst King Mahendra dissolved Parliament on 15 December 1960 and later banned political parties, the communist movement found itself at the crossroads: whether to support the king's move, or to forge ahead with a struggle against absolute monarchy. It is said that Rayamajhi, who was in Moscow participating

[11] In an article in the *International Herald Tribune*, reprinted in the *Kathmandu Post*, it has been argued that no substantial proof exists on Khrushchev actually thumping his shoes at the UN General Assembly in 1960.

in the World Communist Conference at that time, issued a statement in favour of the King having 'taken a progressive step'. But the CPN Politburo under the leadership of Pushpalal opposed it as 'armed terror' and demanded 'a conference of all parliamentary parties'. When Rayamajhi returned in January 1961, demands for party freedom, release of political prisoners, and for fundamental rights were forwarded, but very little was said about the already dissolved Parliament.[12] A month later, a central plenum of the party was organized in Darbhanga, India. The meeting, culminating in a tedious month-long political debate, ultimately came out with three major strategic thrusts: first, in favour of constitutional monarchy led by the Rayamajhi group; second, in favour of reconvening the dissolved Parliament and initiating a united mass movement led by Pushpalal; and third, preferring an election for a Constituent Assembly led by Mohan Bikram Singh. This divergence became more acute as Pushpalal and his associates held their own convention in 1968, leading to the formation of a separate party. Likewise, Mohan Bikram Singh held his independent Fourth Party Congress in September 1974 in India. A third faction too organized a unity conference and declared a Communist Party of its own in 1978, resulting in a motley crowd of a dozen leftist parties in the country.

Naturally, with a wide and complex assortment of diverse individuals with their varied interests and 'ideologies', the overall impact and influence of the leftist movement in the country as a whole was considerably reduced. This trend grew as even this multiple array of leftist leaders was further divided into and nicknamed like 'pro-Soviet', 'pro-China', 'pro-India', 'revisionist', 'pro-palace' by one another.

The break up of the communist movement was primarily triggered by the Sino-Soviet communist split and by the developments taking place in neighbouring India's communist movement. The CPI, which was established on 26 December 1925 in Kanpur with a view to fight for national independence and socialism, resulted in significant historical developments at home and

[12] History of the Communist Party of Nepal CPN (UML): www.cpnuml.org

abroad.[13] During the early years of independence, the CPI won several seats in Parliament. However, during the Seventh Congress of the CPI held in Calcutta [Kolkata] from 31 October to 7 November 1964, the CPI(M) was born as a result of differences in the communist movement at the international and national levels, 'in order to defend the scientific and revolutionary tenets of Marxism-Leninism and its appropriate application in the concrete Indian conditions'.[14] This would obviously impact on other communist groupings as in Nepal, where senior leftist leaders like Man Mohan Adhikari not only had their education in India, but also looked closely to happenings in Indian communist blocs with great interest and attention.

In this context, Marxist thinking, however precise in itself, tends to have a hybrid character assisting Nepal's leftist parties, which have set forth different versions of the Marxist theory to suit each ones interest in the given time period. The term 'ideology' itself is a rather difficult one to define satisfactorily, but it generally conveys the sense of a collective representation of ideas and experience as opposed to the material reality on which experience is based. It does not necessarily refer to the system of values held or put in circulation by the ruling class to establish consensus in the society. Nor is it necessarily a 'false consciousness', a phrase used by Engels. It has, however, been used frequently by Marxists in both senses. Part of the difficulty comes from the fact that Marx and Engels offered different definitions of 'ideology' over a period in which their ideas developed significantly.[15]

It will be worthwhile to restrict our probe to the first faction led by Mohan Bikram Singh only, a firebrand student leader-turned-communist theorist and mass organizer, still underground but always in the news. Singh, son of a wealthy village feudal from rural Pyuthan district of mid-western Nepal, had gained

[13] www.cpofindia.org

[14] www.cpim.org

[15] David Forgacs, 'Modern Literary Theory: A Comparative Study', in *Marxist Literary Theories*, ed. Ann Jefferson and David Robey, London: B.T. Batsford, 1986.

popularity after he destroyed most of the property documents and bond papers held by his father and went on to distribute them to poor peasants. He had commanded a fairly large section of radical leftist young Turks, primarily in the districts which are now strongholds of the CPN(Maoist). In fact, according to many, it was Singh who had done the meticulous groundwork both in terms of propaganda and cadre mobilization, first as a leader of the Fourth Convention, and later as a General Secretary of the CPN(Masal) for a people's armed revolt in this area. Maoists went on to hijack this area from his grip much later. Mohan Bikram had propounded the idea of struggling for a Constituent Assembly as far back as 1961, a fact that is interesting to note in the context of the Maoists taking up the issue 40 years later. In a rare interview to *Rajdhani* daily, Singh discloses:

> The 3rd general convention of our party had approved the idea of a constituent assembly and it remained a major theme for discussion until the 6th general convention. But, the Maoists were initially against the constituent assembly scheme as they viewed it as [a] rightist revisionist slogan. Today, they themselves are in support of the constituent assembly.[16]

During the course of the same interview, the 64-year-old leader revealed that the royalists and the Maoists both want to scrap the present democracy in the country, and the demand for a Constituent Assembly fits exactly into the overall strategy for an authoritarian regime.

By 1985, the Fourth Convention had split, with Nirmal Lama commanding the party and Singh establishing a new platform of extreme left ideology named the CPN(Masal). Dr Baburam Bhattarai too, had previously been associated with Masal group. However, the group broke up in less than two years, and a new revolutionary 'Mashal' was launched, headed by Bhakta Bahadur Shrestha together with Kiran Vaidya and Pushpa Kamal Dahal, alias 'Prachanda', the current chairman of the CPN(Maoist).

[16] 'Youth Flee Villages in Fear of Resurgence of Violence', *Rajdhani*, 29 July 2003, p. 1.

Before we come back to the stormy years of the late 1980s, a look at the internal political equation will help us to understand why, the stimulus of the political parties failed to make an impact on the general populace after all. And then, there will be an attempt to probe Mohan Bikram Singh and the extreme left movement.

CONSOLIDATION OF THE PANCHAYAT

It must not be overlooked that amidst all these confusing developments in the sphere of the left political movement, a tactful King Mahendra and his son King Birendra (who ascended the throne in 1972), first, with his known shrewdness in managing political complexities, and second, with his great interest in foreign affairs, had built up cordial relations with both China and the Soviet Union. The latter assisted Nepal in setting up several industries, including the Janakpur cigarette factory, a portion of the east-west highway, the Birgunj sugar factory, etc., while India's humiliating defeat in a war with China paved the way for Nepal to restructure its relations with its two neighbours by improving its bargaining power *vis-à-vis* both.

The regional situation had turned more favourable for the King's direct rule after 1962. Kathmandu may well have received the kind of inferred promises from New Delhi that it had been seeking as against some of the NC rebels who had fled to India after the royal takeover. Not surprisingly, the NC resistance movement was suspended in November 1962 and then terminated in December by Suvarna Shumsher, on the advice of the Indian government. Moreover, the Panchayat system attracted some of the top leaders, both of the NC and the CPN, notably Dr Tulsi Giri, Biswo Bandu Thapa, Sri Bhadra Sharma (all three former General Secretaries of the NC), along with Dr Keshar Jung Rayamajhi (General Secretary of the CPN), Kamal Raj Regmi (former CPN Member of Parliament) and Shailendra Kumar Upadhyaya (member of the first central committee). The King's personal charisma and hold over the people of the country, with the Panchayat's special focus on nationalism as an essential political slogan, also prevented the leftists from making inroads. Additionally, the late

B.P. Koirala's lifelong dislike of tying up with the communists for a struggle against the Panchayat made the palace the sole benefactor. During these years, both internal and external factors were not conducive to any type of communist uprising in the country.

But the year 1967 was an exception. With the construction of the Kodari highway, gradually, the poor people of the districts of Kavre and Sindhupalchowk (through which this road runs until it terminates in Kodari) had been inspired to wear the badges of Chairman Mao Tse-tung. These badges were being freely brought from Tibet and were becoming more of a fashion. Kathmandu's administration was particularly annoyed as the youngsters in the capital city too began pinning these badges on their coats and reading *Quotations from Chairman Mao.* Being the heyday of the great Cultural Revolution in China and fearing a spread of Mao's revolutionary guidelines, Kathmandu, in turn, started circulating badges with King Mahendra's profile on them.

The situation turned nasty on 1 July 1967 as some members of the youth wing of the banned the NC (including Ram Chandra Poudel, who later became speaker of the lower house of Parliament) broke into the Chinese photo stall inside the Exhibition Compound at Bhrikuti Mandap and the library of the Nepal–China Friendship Association in Kathmandu, shouted anti-China slogans, and demanded the taking down of the portrait of Chairman Mao. The incident annoyed Peking so much that it ordered its ambassador to Nepal, Yang Kung-su, to lodge a serious protest with His Majesty's Government of Nepal. The wording of the protest is uncharacteristic of the courteous Chinese diplomatic etiquette. Till date this protest note remains the only document where the Chinese have used such harsh language against the Government of Nepal:

> This anti-China incident is a great insult to the Chinese people and a gross encroachment on the Chinese diplomatic privileges. The anti-China incident was planned by US imperialism and Indian reactionaries and was approved and supported by the Nepalese government. The reactionary forces in the Nepalese government which are trailing behind imperialism, revisionism and the reactionaries are itching for action. The great socialist

China is not to be trifled with. In conducting anti-China activities, imperialism, revisionism and the reactionaries will break their own skulls. Those who follow them in their anti-China campaign will suffer from the consequences of their own actions.[17]

Following these sporadic incidents, Kathmandu was almost sure that communism, even without outside support, was like a fast-spreading disease and had to be dealt with firmly. To thwart Nepalese youth from being fascinated with this daydream, the Panchayat ministry was geared up, intelligence units strengthened, publications highlighting the salient elements of the Panchayat system brought out, and an understanding was reached with the UK and the US to strengthen the Royal Nepal Army's (RNA's) capability in both logistics and training. An agreement was also reached with the GOI on the supply of arms to the RNA.

JHAPA MOVEMENT

A full decade later, the influence of communism began to trouble the Nepalese administration yet again. Charu Majumdar, a doctrinaire, and founder of the Naxalite movement, broke away from the Communist Party of India (Marxist) and established the Communist Party of India (Marxist-Leninist). The hard-line communist thinkers from West Bengal and Majumdar along with Kanu Sanyal decided to implement the thoughts and dreams of the oppressed class through an armed struggle.

In Naxalbari, West Bengal, an outcaste youth named Wimal Kesan, having received a judicial order, went to plough his land on 2 March 1967 where he was attacked by the gangsters of local landlords. Thus was born the 'Naxalbari' movement. This one incident made the name famous throughout the subcontinent as 'the Naxalvadi [or Naxalite] movement'.

The guns of Naxalbari directed against exploitation and in the name of social development pointed towards the landlords were now turned against bureaucrats, and thus and the Naxalite movement grew.

[17] *Xinhua* reports on the events in Kathmandu on 1 July 1967; Peking, 8 July 1967, p. 1.

The CPI(M-L) first organized several armed uprisings of landless agricultural labourers, especially in eastern India in 1967, but it speedily developed into an urban guerrilla movement, notably in Kolkata. The Indian government tried to suppress these terror campaigns with superior armed strength resulting in considerable violence. This presented multiple dilemmas for neighbouring Nepal. Hundreds of Nepalese students were studying in West Bengal who could have slowly got involved with the fascinating philosophy of Majumdar, which they could experiment with back home. The Nepalese districts neighbouring West Bengal were particularly vulnerable.

Influenced by the developments in the neighbouring West Bengal, major turmoil emerged in the communist movement of Nepal in 1974 when the Jhapa District Committee of the East Koshi Zonal Committee revolted and started an armed struggle. With the central slogan of 'attack the class enemy', mainly influenced by the Chinese Cultural Revolution and the Indian Naxalite movement. This action critically threatened the capitalist, feudal upper class and upper-middle class of the eastern province of the kingdom. C.P. Mainali, R.K. Mainali, Mohan Chandra Adhikari, etc., were the foremost revolutionaries masterminding the ruthless killing of at least seven people in Jhapa, an eastern, politically vulnerable district of Nepal. Predictably, the Panchayati administration's counteraction was extreme. Dozens of these 'revolutionaries' were arrested while others were forced to flee to India. But due to its scale and the massive publicity of the incident, the Jhapa movement greatly influenced other potential revolutionaries-to-be, specially students.

The consequences were evident: stories of the 'heroic Mainali brothers' and their inspirational deeds proliferated, much to the dismay of not only the government, but even other leftist leaders who were, by this time, slowly losing their mass appeal with their old, in some ways redundant, strategies of revolution. The fascination of the Jhapa action broadened its base, and ultimately culminated in a separate Marxist-Leninist line within the communist movement of Nepal. In 1974, the Jhapa District Committee and the Nepal Revolutionary Organization, Morang, issued a joint appeal on the basis of four preconditions for the coordination of revolutionaries and revolutionary groups. By June 1975, the revolutionary groups and workers had agreed upon the preconditions, organized an underground conference, and had already formed the All Nepal Communist Revolutionary Coordination Committee (Marxist-Leninist). Later, the Liberation Front, Revolutionary Communist Organizing Committee of Gandaki as well as the 'Shandesh Group' joined in. The CPN(M-L) was established on 26 December 1978 by a conference held by the group. A virtual wave of unification followed, as a result of which, the CPN(M-L) developed as the most influential party in the communist movement of Nepal.[18]

Leftist students were very much part of the mass protest on 6 April 1979 at the Pakistani embassy in Kathmandu against President Zia-ul Haq's decision to hang Zulfikar Ali Bhutto. Riot police clashed with students, resulting in the closure of campuses in Kathmandu and in other major cities. Since the Nepal Police did not even have tear gas shells till then, these were imported hastily from Singapore to suppress an increasing number of agitators, even in comparatively peaceful towns like Hetauda. An agreement was reached between the government and student organizations affiliated with the Congress and the communist faction of the Pushpalal group. A more radical Mohan Bikram Singh's communist bloc decided, however, to denounce the agreement. Hence, it can be seen that Singh's faction (from which the current Maoist party emerged) has always followed a radical line. Those students who signed this accord were termed as traitors and paraded around the city with painted faces. One of them was Bal Bahadur K.C., the erstwhile Minister for Tourism and Civil Aviation. As the demonstrations turned ugly with the attempted torching of Gorkhapatra (the country's official newspaper publishing house) and the Royal Nepal Airlines Corporation's buildings, King Birendra announced on 24 May 1979 that a referendum based on adult franchise would be held in order to find the choice of the people whether to retain the partyless

[18] Communist Party of Nepal (United Marxist-Leninist): www.cpnuml.org

Panchayat system with suitable reforms, or set up a multiparty system of governance.

While the banned NC was all set on campaigning for the re-establishment of the multiparty system, the leftist blocs were initially unsure of what to do: whether to boycott the referendum, or to vote in support of the multiparty polity. They had been moderately amenable to programmes like 'back to the villages' under the Panchayat system that somewhat resembled the Cultural Revolution to them. However, even Mohan Bikram Singh, along with Man Mohan Adhikari, Tulsi Lal, Sahana Pradhan, and Narayan Man Bijukchhe embarked on garnering public support for the success of the multiparty system. Except for Singh, the others took part in mass meetings and door-to-door campaigns. When voting finally took place in May 1980, the reformed Panchayat system triumphed, with most of the districts in the village turning massively in its favour over the multiparty system. B.P. Koirala, a legendary leader famous for his broad-heartedness and statesmanship, admitted defeat.

This was an opportunity for the Panchayat to streamline its efforts, focusing on uplifting the living standards of the poor and the underprivileged (specially in the rural areas), and there was renewed expectation of a concerted endeavour to check corruption, stop injustice to the poor by the ruling elite, and punishment to those who had been responsible for harming the innocent. It was also an opportunity to harness national vigour and synergy for the all-round development of the country. Nepal's communist movement, which perpetually lacked revolutionary leadership and had a tendency of revisionism and constantly confused the masses with flowery phrases and speeches, therefore, failed to ignite the masses. During the 10 years after the referendum, there was a sustained effort to garner international support for Nepal's economic uplift. New avenues for export promotion, earning foreign currency, and active participation in regional organizations like SAARC and international organizations like the UN and NAM boosted Nepal's image of independence in the international arena. It was during this phase that tourism became the country's economic backbone. Today, many people look back with nostalgia at the fact that the Concorde of Air France and 747 Jumbo jets of Air Canada landed at Tribhuvan international airport, while Lufthansa and Singapore Airlines began operating in Nepal, both of which stopped their flights, citing financial losses in the ensuing decade.

END OF PANCHAYAT SYSTEM

Despite this progress in national and international forums, Indo-Nepal relations regrettably faced an all-time low by the end of the 1980s. Insiders referred to the deliberate lapse of trade and transit treaties with India as a direct consequence of the clash between New Delhi and Kathmandu. Some others pointed to the erosion of personal relations between HM King Birendra and Prime Minister Rajiv Gandhi and between late Queen Aishwarya and Mrs Sonia Gandhi. Whatever the case, the Nepalese people faced tremendous hardship due to the unavailability of even the daily essentials like kerosene, petrol and diesel as prices skyrocketed. Initially, the Panchayat did try to whip up nationalistic (read anti-Indian) sentiments. Even today, this particular decision of the GOI is viewed as a perfect example of 'India's high-handedness over its small and vulnerable neighbours'. But slowly Nepalese populace got fed up with the futility of queuing up in endless kerosene and petrol lines, and ultimately turned against the Panchayat itself.

The collapse of communist governments in the whole of eastern Europe, the mass uprising in Tiananmen Square in Beijing, and a worldwide progression towards multiparty democracy helped the NC in planning a mass movement against the 30 years of partyless rule. This came as a blessing in disguise for the NC. Its supreme leader Ganesh Man Singh was accommodative of the leftist parties and did not regard it as a taboo to join hands with communists like B.P. Koirala. The Indian leadership, including Chandrashekhar, had also counselled Singh that it would be the correct decision to make under the circumstances to join hands with the leftist forces.

The interim period is one of the most tumultuous in the country's history. The Fourth Congress of the CPN was conducted underground by the CPN(M-L) in August 1989 in Siraha district. The important outcomes of this meet were the laying down of concrete policies, principles, and programmes for a joint mass movement against the partyless Panchayat system. It also put forth the new ideological viewpoint that a multiparty framework should be adopted within the communist political thought, a unique line in itself for a leftist political force. Madan Bhandari, a fire-brand mass organizer, became its general secretary. The Congress, in addition, formed a joint mass movement group comprising the CPN(M-L), CPN(Marxist), CPN(Fourth Congress), Nepal Workers' and Peasants' Party, CPN(Verma), CPN(Amatya), and CPN (Manandhar). It also launched what was called a 'functional unity' with the NC, another landmark decision having long-term consequences for Nepalese politics. Here, it will be worthwhile to come back to the CPN(Masal) and CPN(Mashal) discussed earlier. These parties, including the Nepal Communist League, did not join the joint mass movement group along with the other left parties. The NC, instead, formed a separate mass movement organizing committee: a strong reason for the Congress later calling them 'anti-democratic' and 'pro-palace'. Their choice of struggling for democracy and 'total revolution' without aligning with the main political forces has never quite been understood even by other left parties. However, their group organized a few 'Masal rallies', and was primarily responsible for vandalizing police booths in and around Kathmandu, but nothing significant in comparison to the contribution of the NC and other left parties to oust the Panchayat.

Though the mass movement was brief (18 February 1990 to 8 April 1990), its success was sudden and extraordinary. It is well-known that the uprising was centred around the main cities, specially Kathmandu, where thousands took to the streets and demanded an end to the Panchayat system. Teachers, lawyers, doctors, housewives and students set up road blocks, burnt tyres and effigies, shouted slogans and clashed with police. Even though the Mallik Commission report does not cite more than two people dead in front of the royal palace on 6 April 1990, it is true that the RNA was brought out to disperse the crowd of one hundred thousand followed by two days of curfew. King Birendra, through a royal proclamation on 8 April, lifted the ban on political parties. The Masal and Mashal at this point went on to denounce the tripartite agreement, and even criticised the Constitution of the Kingdom of Nepal brought out later that year.[19]

The people's movement of 1990 is significant in two important aspects as we study the growth of Nepal's leftism: for the first time, leftist political parties (including the most radical ones) were thrown into competitive politics and were now allowed to operate in the open; and they had now savoured the taste of a mass uprising in the form of a revolution which they imagined could be moulded and further advanced on the road to a full-fledged socialist people's republic.

A NEW DEMOCRATIC ORDER

State, system, and politics definitely entered a new phase in conforming to the true desires of the people and resolving the misery prevalent in Nepalese society for centuries. In fact, the leaders of the same generation who had struggled to bring in democracy in the kingdom in 1950 were the ones at the helm of affairs after the success of the people's movement in 1990, re-establishing a democratic political structure that was accepted all over the world as the finest. The Constitution of 1990, a tripartite union of the palace, the NC, and the communist bloc, recognized Parliament as the legitimate mirror of the will of the sovereign people, a non-partisan constitutional monarchy that would be the guardian of the Constitution, the government accountable to Parliament, a free and fair judiciary, a free press, a non-political bureaucracy, and the Army.[20] The Nepalese, in general, were now hopeful that the new group of dedicated leaders who had

[19] Hari Sharma, 'Popular Mobilization and Emergence of Collective Identity in Nepal's Transition to Democracy–1990', *Nepali Journal of Contemporary Studies*, vol. 1, 2001, p. 22.

[20] See The Constitution of the Kingdom of Nepal, 1990.

struggled for decades, would take the nation on the right path by focusing on the country's overall welfare and economic development. Much also depended on the unwritten rules of the game. Sincerity, honesty, dedication are, in fact, dependent to a large extent on the political actors who emerge on the scene to rule the nation. Developmental plans and programmes too are reliant on the eagerness to implement them. Lifeless words of the Constitution themselves do not guarantee corruption-free governance. Good governance itself is subject to the stability of the government, while the governments in power have to satisfy the personal requirements of the members of the Parliament.

Soon after the promulgation of the Constitution, a split took place within the United Left Front. On 10 December 1990, four components of the front, viz., the Amatya Group, the Verma Group, the Workers' and Peasants' Party led by Rohit, and the Fourth Convention group led by Nirmal Lama withdrew their support and the Front subsequently ceased to exist. However, efforts to forge a broader unity among the left parties continued so that they could contest the 1991 elections jointly.[21] But less than a month later, the CPN(Marxist) led by Sahana Pradhan and Man Mohan Adhikari merged with the CPN(M-L), giving a new name to the party, CPN(United Marxist-Leninist). After the declaration of general elections, there were altogether 44 parties applying for registration before the Election Commission. Among these, the following 14 were parties with leftist leanings.

CPN(UML); CPN(Verma); CPN(Manandhar); CPN(Amatya); CPN(Masal); CPN(Sixth Convention); CPN(Janamukhi); Nepal Communist League; Nepal Communist Sanghathan; Nepal Terai Communist Party; Nepal Marxist-Leninist Party; Nepal Workers' and Peasants' Party; Samyukta Janmorcha Nepal; Nepal Communist Party (Unity Centre).[22]

With this diverse assortment of communist parties contesting

[21] Krishna P. Khanal, 'Party Politics and Governance: The Role of Leadership', in *State, Leadership and Politics in Nepal*, ed. Dhruba Kumar, Kathmandu: Centre for Nepal and Asian Studies, 1995, p. 53.

[22] The Election Commission of Nepal.

the elections, the voters, naturally, were placed in a state of confusion and indecisiveness. Furthermore, on the international scene, the fall of communism in the countries of eastern Europe and the collapse of the Soviet Union came as an impediment to Nepalese leftist forces, as they were already facing spoofs and satires from the NC and other rightist and centrist parties as being 'out-of-date' and having received a hard smack from the people of the eastern European countries.

With all these varied national and international developments, the second general election after the success of the *jan andolan* [people's movement] affirmed the following results (see Table 1.1).

With 65 per cent turnout, there was a clear sign that the people preferred the two major parties that had led the struggle of 1990. They elected the NC to form the government, and wanted the CPN (UML) to check the doings of the government as the main opposition in Parliament. Although Pyuthan, Rolpa, and other districts with strong Masal (Mohan Bikram Singh's party) leanings reported voting as low as 36 per cent, there was little impact of ultra-leftist influence on the country's electorate, except, of course, the nine seats that the UPF succeeded in capturing, plus two in the upper house.

A note on the UPF will add to our overview of the period that culminated with the start of the Maoist movement in 1996. Soon after the advent of multiparty democracy, Nirmal Lama's CPN

TABLE 1.1: PARTY POSITION IN THE LOWER HOUSE AFTER 1991 ELECTIONS

Party	Seats
Nepali Congress	110
CPN(UML)	69
United People's Front	9
Nepal Sadhvabana Party	6
National Democratic Party (Chand)	3
National Democratic Party (Thapa)	1
CPN(Democratic)	2
NWP Party	2

(Fourth Convention), Bhakta Bahadur's CPN(Mashal), and Rup Lal Biswokarma's Workers' Organization united to form what they called the 'CPN(Unity Centre)', with Comrade Prachanda as its general secretary. Later, Haribol Gajurel and Dr Baburam Bhattarai too entered the Centre from the CPN(Janmukhi) and CPN(Masal) of Mohan Bikram Singh respectively. The party floated a political wing called the 'United People's Front' (UPF), which they allowed to contest the parliamentary elections mentioned above. Its MPs officially joined the multiparty electorate process 'to reveal to the people the futility of parliamentary democracy and to employ it as a stepping stone towards establishing a new people's republic'. The Unity Centre held its first national conference in 1992, in which the proposal for a protracted armed struggle on the route to a new democratic revolution was discussed and accepted.

By 1994, the Unity Centre was divided into two factions—the first led by Nirmal Lama and the second by Prachanda. Reflecting that split, the UPF too fell apart with the group that supported Prachanda led by Dr Baburam Bhattarai. Both factions approached the Election Commission, but the one which supported Nirmal Lama was given recognition. Dr Bhattarai then called for a boycott of the elections, an action that at that time was perceived more as a face-saving measure.[23]

He also wrote a letter to Parliament saying that the MPs of the UPF (now of Nirmal Lama's group) should be stripped of their membership. Even before the split, the MPs of the UPF did nothing inside Parliament that could be termed unparliamentary, thus indubitably vesting the entire state of affairs to the style of functioning of the government of the Nepali Congress Party with Girija Prasad Koirala as the prime minister. In a nutshell, the following are the major turning points in the course of the final formation of the CPN(Maoist).

1974: Mohan Bikram Singh organizes the Fourth Convention and formalizes the NCP split. The Maoists are latter-day offshoots of this stream.

[23] Deepak Thapa, 'The Origin', *Probe* (Dhaka), vol. 1, issue 12, p. 15.

1983: Singh's NCP(Masal) splits again: softer leftists stay with Nirmal Lama. Hardliners split again; Mohan Baidya walks away with those believing in Mao-style revolution and forms the NCP(Mashal).

1989: Pushpa Kamal Dahal (Comrade Prachanda) takes over as general secretary of the Mohan Baidya stream.

1990: NCP(Mashal), Nirmal Lama's faction, and other smaller groups come together to form the Ekata Kendra (Unity Centre). Masal decides to boycott general elections, so Baburam Bhattarai joins the Unity Centre, which wins nine seats in the 1991 polls to become the third-largest party in Parliament. The United General Conference which was convened the same year approved Prachanda's plan to launch a 'people's war' and outvoted Nirmal Lama's 'mass uprising' line.

1992: The Unity Centre fares badly in local-government elections, and the party formally has a name change to 'CPN(Maoist)'.

1994: The CPN(Mashal) splits again. The Election Commission did not recognize the faction led by Baburam Bhattarai and the Maoists, approving, instead, the United People's Front. The 'optionless' Maoists boycotted the 1994 mid-term polls. Later the court rules that Bhattarai's was the legitimate party, but it was too late.

13 February 1996: The United People's Front of Baburam Bhattarai submits a list of 40 demands to Prime Minister Sher Bahadur Deuba that it wanted met by 17 February. But the Maoists went on the offensive four days before the deadline, attacking the police posts at Rukum, Rolpa, Gorkha, and Sindhuli.[24]

The Tanakpur agreement reached with India on Koirala's visit to India in December 1991 escalated into a highly controversial issue, fuelled by the entire Nepalese left including the main opposition party and the UPF. They alleged that the agreement of the project didn't allow Nepal either adequate share of water for irrigation, or the electricity that it generated. The United People's Front likewise contested the local elections in May 1992,

[24] Binod Bhattarai, 'Prachanda's Warpath', *Nepali Times* (Kathmandu), 30 November–6 December 2001, p. 6.

tying up with Masal, Rohit's NWPP, the CPN(Marxist, Leninist, Maoist), CPN(15 September) and the Nepal Communist League. It succeeded in winning 5 per cent of the seats in Village Development Committees, but its influence was considerably higher in areas such as Pyuthan, Rolpa, and Salyan.

As a result, the focus inevitably ceased to be on the struggle of political parties against the palace: instead, what arose was the difficulty of governing the nation in accordance with the wishes of the people. As a matter of fact, most of the political leaders who came to occupy senior posts had little experience in administrative matters as they were in hideouts, prisons, or in exile in India. Now the question of the leaders' own commitments to translate mass preferences into public policies arose as the people demanded solutions to all their woes and difficulties.

Naturally, as in other emerging democracies, managing a democratic change was an onerous task, specially as Nepal is plagued with—among other predicaments—massive poverty, unemployment, lack of resources, illiteracy, and an extremely difficult terrain. Moreover, an increasing consciousness of identity led to ethnic groups (particularly the *janjatis*) to press their demands more vigorously. The assumption (which has been proved wrong on many occasions) was of top-down programmes framed by the centralized government planning machinery assuming that villagers are illiterate and their assessment of needs has to be prepared in the capital of the country. This led to a substantial part of the national resources going to the districts of political heavyweights influencing decision-making at the centre, and development works in other areas (notably in the mid-western region) were neglected. A regular custom during the reign of the Panchayat was that the late King and Queen used to visit each of the five development regions every winter, to look into the development projects of the government and assessing the demands of the people, and keeping in touch with the common folk of the villages. The politicians in power, and the prime minister heading the government failed to do this in subsequent years.

Koirala recommended the dissolution of the house for a snap

poll in 1994. It resulted in a hung Parliament, with the CPN(UML) forming a minority government as the largest party in the house. Man Mohan Adhikari, a lifelong fighter for democratic values and principles and a relentless yet unpretentious communist became the prime minister. He may well have been successful, but he did not have enough time. With the National Democratic Party and the NC coming closer together, he was forced into dissolving the house again after just about nine months in power. Several analysts agree that the public image of the UML was saved from being stained like that of the NC with this limited time in government.

It is said that there is no other dilemma for a revolutionary leftist than when a fellow Marxist-Leninist is in the government. The United People's Front presented a 39-point list of demands to the UML Government in 1995 consisting of a range of issues from nationalism to the concerns of the daily life of the man on the street. The government gave an assurance that it would look into the points put forward in the petition. During the tenure of Sher Bahadur Deuba, they once again presented a 40-point petition in February 1996, leading to a manifestation of a conflict which has till date taken nearly twelve thousand lives.

CHAPTER 2

Start of the Maoist War

Comrade Prachanda, in an interview to Li Onesto of *Revolutionary Worker*, stated that there was already a heated debate within the Unity Centre to initiate the people's war in the country even as its front organization, the United People's Front, had nine MPs in Parliament in 1995.[1] He reveals:

> Making the plan for the commencement of the struggle, there was a great debate over how to go to the armed struggle because many people were influenced by peaceful struggle, work in the parliament, rightist and petty bourgeois feelings and a long tradition of the reformist movement. Then we said that the only process must be a big push, a big leap. Not gradual change.

True to his statement, in March 1995, the Unity Centre held what it named, its Third Plenum, during which parliamentary elections were denounced and a decision was taken to take up arms against the existing state.

What, then, was the 40-point list of demands submitted by Dr Baburam Bhattarai to the then Sher Bahadur Deuba Government on 4 February 1996, nine days after which the party decided to go for a people's revolutionary war. It can be said with certainty that there was precise thinking and a thorough agenda to 'take the big leap' even prior to forwarding the petition to the Deuba Government. Therefore, the petition may have been submitted purely for publicity purposes and laying the grounds for the armed struggle. This supposition is supported by the fact that, contrary to the covering letter of the 40-point list of demands which had mentioned that 'unless the government initiated positive steps towards fulfilling those demands by 17 February 1996, we will be

[1] *Revolutionary Worker*, vol. 1043, 20 February 2000, p. 1.

forced to embark on an armed struggle against the existing state', they instead chose to strike in six districts four days earlier. Prime Minister Deuba was at that time on an official visit to India. This writer was part of the PM's entourage to Delhi. There was actually no news with the journalists of the Maoists taking up arms either at the Ashoka Hotel where the entourage stayed during the interaction programmes or at other functions.

Sir Robert Thompson, in his book *Defeating Communist Insurgency*, has outlined, '...every Communist insurgency needs a cause and for this reasoning every effort is given to adopt causes which appear catchy, progressive but difficult to obtain'. Accordingly, anti-colonialism was the primary slogan of the communists in the late 1950s and early 1960s. The dominant cause in Vietnam in the summer of 1965 was to drive out the Americans. The demand for a republic is the last that Nepal, as a state, can surrender to. Hence, populist slogans help while appealing and making clear, not so much to the intellectuals of the cities, but to the unemployed and illiterate youth of the rural areas 'that the revolution is going to be long and harsh'. Says Thomson, 'when times are hard and food is short, the inevitability of final, decisive victory has always been a strong card to play', and communist revolutionaries all over the world make it a point to make demands that the state cannot easily fulfil.

It is difficult to analyse what would have happened if the then government had outright accepted to consider 38 out of the 40 demands or instituted a high-level committee to debate the issues put forth by Dr Baburam Bhattarai. It may be worthwhile to scrutinize the 40-point list handed over to PM Deuba just before his official visit to India (see Annexure I).

It is interesting to note that whereas the point number 10 the charter of demands has called for the drafting of a new constitution for a republican state, the following point calls only 'for the special prerogatives of the King and the royal family to be abolished'. Points number 25 and 37, although desirable, call for something that is almost impossible for any government to fulfil even in a time period of, say, a decade, whereas various governments have already moved in the direction of executing points number 19 and 27 as they are attached with the sentiments of a large section of the populace. Points 1–5 are directly connected with Nepal's relations with India. Points 10 and 11 are not possible to fulfil, as the government itself does not have the authority to do so according to the existing Constitution. But let us presume hypothetically, that the Deuba Government had instituted a high-level task force to look into the demands. Would the armed movement then have been stalled? It would have definitely embarrassed them as they had already decided on launching the movement, because in March 1995, Prachanda's Unity Centre had held its Third Plenum, during which they had decided to take up arms.

The Maoists applied the same theories that the masters of guerrilla warfare like Guevara, Mao, Sun-Tzu and Giap had applied and preached (see Annexure II). Parallels have been drawn to the techniques of warfare adopted by Mao or Guevara, *vis-à-vis* the unique terrain of Nepal, its distinct geopolitical location, and the changed international context since their time.

With these important and interesting theories, we shall proceed to the evolution of the Maoist movement; its gradual hardening; its success in marginalizing the government's rural administration; its triumph in developing base areas in Rolpa, Rukum, Salyan, Pyuthan, and Jajarkot; and ultimately turning into a virtual alternate to the Nepali state. Not all the developments, bomb blasts and operations that take place almost on a weekly basis have been listed or analysed in this monograph. What is important is not the mundane detail, but examination of the pattern of how it has been progressing, and how it is likely to advance in the coming days.

CHAPTER 3

Basic Causes Behind the Growth of the Insurgency

Not every country with a high rate of unemployment, illiteracy, corruption, centralized administrative structure, and political instability harbours a violent communist insurgency. The basic cause behind the Maoist rebellion has always bewildered Kathmandu's elite and the donor community. Dozens of articles have been written suggesting one or the other explanation, but none gives a perceptive *raison d'être* behind the actual motivation or the sources of the rebellion. It is probably a combination of the reasons listed and analysed below which may have assisted the Maoists in gathering momentum for their rebellion.

POLITICAL INSTABILITY

The change of the political system in 1990 aroused expectations among the general population, both in urban and rural areas. While the people were exercising their new-found freedom to speak out, strikes/demonstrations/rallies/*bandhs* have been characteristic of the post-democracy stage. Among the rural folk, it was definitely a frustrating experience, as they saw that the very fundamentals of living were not being met by the state despite having changed from an autocratic to a democratic order. As mushrooming political parties entered the rural districts to request for votes for the elections of 1991, the Nepalese had a dream: powerful, emotive, amorphous and embryonic. They knew that the leaders had spent most of their lives in prison and that most of them were in pitiable economic conditions themselves, hence, it was but natural for the people to compare their own state of abject poverty with that of their leaders.

However, the performance of the first democratically elected government after 1990 was not satisfactory. Governments of dissimilar political parties, diverse political equations, and bizarre formations began to appear and fall apart.[1] In the last 12 years, there is no experiment that the Nepali political landscape has not tested: majority governments, a minority government, coalition governments, and a minority single-party government, yet, democracy failed to live up to the expectations of many, as in eastern Europe, where authoritarian regimes of a different kind fell at about the same time.

One may question why the people of Japan or Italy don't resort to arms with such frequent changes in their governments. Perhaps the key difference is that as soon as there is a change in the government in Nepal, secretaries, ambassadors, planning commission members, even IGPs get their marching orders, resulting in an almost total reversal of policy and programmes and their speed of implementation. Hence, with 12 prime ministers and an equal number of finance and home ministers, the entire focus of governments was naturally on their own stability rather than the welfare of the people. Coupled with the inefficiency and instability of the state administration, the Maoist movement forged ahead with zeal and enthusiasm with urban money through extortion and support from rural area. The tug-of-war for hot seats and factionalism in almost every major political party within the country created politics of confusion and uncertainty with few realizing the damage that was being done to the already weak foundation of democracy.

The extreme left activists in Rolpa and other places had either been imprisoned or killed on the direct orders of Kathmandu, which became another reason for a vendetta. The decision could have been successful at nipping the insurgency in the bud, but without popular backing and lacking moral and legal sustenance, it was only to backfire.

[1] Nishchal Nath Pandey, 'Nepal: Democracy Taking Roots', in *India and Nepal*, Embassy of India in Nepal, 2002, p. 20.

The hopes of the people were belied by the same leaders who were expected to make their living conditions better. The plain truth was—now the people started to dream again!

WIDESPREAD CORRUPTION, POVERTY, AND BAD GOVERNANCE

The revolving-door charade of ministers with the formation and fall of different governments only increased corrupt practices across the board. Donors felt obliged to preach democratically elected governments to deliver good governance to the same sovereign people who had voted the leaders to power! Thus, 12 years of misrule, non-performance, and blatant corruption appears to be the principal causes of increasing frustration among the masses, specially the people of the rural hilly areas.

Half of Nepal's population lives in absolute poverty; 80 per cent of the children are thought to be suffering from malnutrition. Literacy is still low despite crores [one crore being equal to 10 million] being poured annually into the education sector. The economy, too which depends mainly on agriculture, is not healthy. Some development indicators actually seem to be in reverse—particularly with respect to women and the girl child—despite almost 40 years of involvement of foreign donors.

Although numerous donor agencies have been advocating a positive change and vying to connect rural areas to knowledge, experience, and resources to help poor people build a better life, it is not certain whether they have actually helped develop local capacity so that the Nepalese could solve their problems by themselves. The districts where the Maoist movement first started have been neglected not only by the state, but by and large also by the donor agencies. Some of the major projects undertaken in Rolpa district, for instance, were the Rapti Development Project from 1987 to 1997 by USAID under the Ministry of Local Development,[2] and the Integrated Development Project in Baglung and Rolpa districts from 1992 to 1997 by DEN/DANIDA under the same ministry. The first project's aim was 'to increase agricultural and forestry production through local capacity building', while the latter's was 'to improve the living conditions for the poorer part of the population of the two districts'. The evolution and achievements of the Maoists in the area prove that these projects were utter failures.

On the other hand, serious concerns over the government's style of functioning and its total lack of seriousness in implementing good governance have time and again provoked severe criticism from donors. A statement presented to Prime Minister Girija Prasad Koirala by a group of donors representing an overwhelming majority of donor agencies working in Nepal stated:

> In the past few years, the role of the political leaders in Nepal has become a major factor in the development of the country. This has happened at a time when the relationship between 'good governance' and development is at the forefront of the domestic agenda as well as the international aid agenda. The essential ingredients of good governance—efficiency, accountability, transparency and the rule of law in government and public administration—are seen as essential to social and economic development and to effective development assistance. In light of their experience in recent years, many donors supporting Nepal, and even the general public in Nepal, have begun to raise this as an urgent matter. Some of these concerns were brought up at the last Nepal Aid Group Meeting held in the spring of 1996. Others have emerged and have grown since then.... Should such progress not be achieved, the donor community sees grave risks for Nepal's future. Their strong view is that only the people of Nepal can ultimately solve the fundamental problems affecting their country today, and that the political leadership bears the key responsibility to renew the reform and development process.[3]

After nearly four years, as they saw that Nepal's successive governments had turned a deaf ear to their appeal, a stronger

[2] Kanak Mani Dixit, publisher of *Himal South Asia*, questioned Peter A. Burleigh, an American diplomat, at a talk programme organized by the Institute of Foreign Affairs on 26 February 2002 that USAID must be knowing more about the causes behind the growth of the Maoist rebellion, as it was involved in development projects in the Rapti zone.

[3] 'Concerns of Nepal's Development Partners', statement presented to Prime Minister Mr G. P. Koirala on 15 May 1998 by a group of donors representing donor agencies working in Nepal.

note was made public at the NDF meet held in Kathmandu during 4–7 February 2002. Although the donors pledged to provide $500 million for poverty alleviation, they made it clear that 'the support however depended on the continued commitment, effective implementation and the results they bring'. They were also concerned about the implementation of related programmes, corruption control, transparency, and good governance.[4]

With the initiative of the UK, an international meet on Nepal was held in London during 19–20 June 2002 to discuss the Maoist situation and the economic assistance that Nepal desperately needed. India and China, both the country's neighbours, sat down together (which in itself was a rare event) to discuss Nepal. According to a press release issued by the British embassy at the conclusion of the assembly, 'the meeting noted that the conflict posed a threat to regional stability and human rights of the people of Nepal and called for urgent need to tackle poverty, exclusion, poor governance, discrimination, corruption, livelihoods and human rights'. However, the Nepalese delegation, which was only allowed to present its national paper at the first session, did not attend the closed-door meeting where the donor community discussed their role in supporting Nepal to combat terrorism and to meet its development challenge. The leader of the Nepalese delegation, Dr Shankar Sharma, on his return to Kathmandu, disclosed that 'the meet made it clear that Nepal will have to curb corruption, enhance efficiency and provide good governance'. He told *Nepal* magazine in an interview that the donors even named some corrupt ministers who were in power.

The 2002 Budget presented by the government headed by Prime Minister Deuba similarly forecast a gloomy economic picture for the country. Out of Rs. 96.12 billion, Rs. 57.45 billion has been set aside for regular expenditure and Rs. 38.68 billion for development. For the first time in history, regular expenses were higher

[4] The Nepal Development Forum held in Kathmandu and Pokhara (4–7 February 2002) was co-chaired by the then Finance Minister Dr Ram Sharan Mahat and Dr Mieko Nishimizu, World Bank Vice President for South Asia. The forum was attended by delegations from 23 countries and international organizations.

than expenditure under the development section in the context of the government deeming law and order more important than poverty alleviation or economic reforms. A whopping Rs. 14 billion was allocated for the security forces.

Corruption in Nepal has indeed become a chronic disease, and although every prime minister has vowed to wipe out taking of commissions and other kinds of corruption, not even a single minister has been convicted and jailed for financial wrong doing in the last 12 years. While the Commission for Investigation on Abuse of Authority (CIAA) has detained a few leading politicians, their cases are still pending in court for final verdict. By and large, corruption in the country possesses the following basic characteristics:

1. Decisions are taken not for public benefit but to serve the interests of a few.[5]
2. High costs, overly complex and prestigious projects are favoured over cost-efficient development projects based on the most relevant technique.
3. The corrupt are not punished, but are instead rewarded and encouraged. Political instability facilitates financial wrong doing, as colossal amounts of money are required to lure MPs of other parties and factions to desert.
4. Elections are becoming extremely costly, hence, it is a widely accepted belief that without black money, elections cannot be won.
5. Human rights abuses have increased as corruption increased. Regimes become more secretive, less tolerant of dissent, and more fearful of loss of power. Basic social and economic rights such as access to medical care, education, adequate shelter and good water are threatened.
6. The larger the bureaucracy, the more the delay and the more the instances of corruption. Even to get a simple thing done, it has become a custom to bribe a public servant simply on the understanding that he/she would do it quickly.

[5] Transparency International Nepal: www.tinepal.org

Even in a place like Bihar, infamous for bad governance and heights of absurdity among its leaders, the chief minister himself was jailed for his alleged involvement in a bribery case. Nepal, on the other hand, has not built institutions efficient, daring and truly independent enough to convict judges, ministers, and prime ministers, an appalling reason for the growing frustration among the people, even with various constitutional establishments supposedly independent of governmental influence.

ALIENATION OF THE MID-WEST AND THE FIGHTING SPIRIT OF THE *JANJATIS* AND THE MAGAR CLAN

The mid-western region where the Maoist movement started is, no doubt, the least developed, most backward and poverty-stricken area of the kingdom with a low level of education, poor health and infrastructure facilities, and an extremely difficult terrain. In terms of land distribution of the whole of the country by development regions, the largest area (28.8 per cent) is covered by this region. It also has the largest forest area (27.39 per cent) in the country. However, there are just 13 hospitals, 9 small airports, and 486 post offices. During the Panchayat period, due attention was given by the Singha Durbar to the development of the far-western region because of its great distance from the relatively well-developed central region (with Kathmandu as the capital) while this area was utterly neglected. Despite the fact that gradually reducing the existing imbalance in interregional and subregional socio-economic zones and developing functional interrelationships between the mid-west and the centre was a national policy, this was never actually implemented.

Even Dr Baburam Bhattarai mentions:

> . . . what [some] term 'law and order' problem is basically a socio-economic problem of extreme poverty and exploitation in the rural areas of Nepal under the present semi-feudal and semi-colonial dispensation. How do [you] expect social peace and harmony to prevail in a socio-political system which increasingly generated poverty, unemployment, illiteracy and all round underdevelopment for more than ninety per cent of the toiling population

in mostly rural areas and filthy richness and extravagance for a handful of parasitic classes in rural and urban areas?[6]

That this extreme poverty sparked off an armed uprising is understandable, but exactly how it took place is difficult to comprehend. This area of the kingdom was also known for its relatively high proportion of marijuana cultivation, the returns from which used to be sufficient to bridge the annual food deficit in the area. However, in 1976 the HMG/N banned the cultivation and sale of hashish and enforced it effectively, generating widespread resentment in the Rapti zone. According to one school of thought, antipathy of the Rapti zone dwellers to the centre had begun right after this decision, much before the CPN(Maoists) were able to penetrate the area.

Likewise, the Sher Bahadur Deuba Committee report too, states that estrangement of the mid-western region was not corrected even after the establishment of the multiparty system. Panchayati leaders who were elected to the Rashtriya Panchayat (National Parliament in the Panchayati era) from the area automatically shifted to the NC, but instead of a concerted effort to address the woes of the people, political parties engaged in games of one-upmanship that benefited only the extreme left ideology.[7] And even though Surendra Hamal was minister of state for labour and transport from Rolpa district, Marichman Singh Shrestha was prime minister for five years during the Panchayat from Salyan, and Gopal Ji Jung Shah was assistant minister for industry from Rukum, the developmental activities in this area had been negligible, almost to the point of being non-existent.

On the contrary, a survey conducted jointl yby the Kathmandu-based ICIMOD and SNV states that 'Rolpa was the 12th worse off out of seventy five districts in the country in overall development, 25th in poverty and deprivation index and 12th according to

[6] Interview to the *Independent*, vol. V, no. 41, 13–19 December 1995, p. 6.

[7] Read the report of the Sher Bahadur Deuba Committee formed to render recommendations on the Maoist Problem by the K.P. Bhattarai Government, 2000, p. 23.

women's empowerment index. Districts further west in the hilly region are characterized by indices, which are even worse.' All the district headquarters of the mid-west region are connected by road. Why then did the Maoist movement evolve and prosper in the mid-west? It has a lot to do with the fighting spirit of the people of the region, as well as a number of other factors.

The Magars, who are predominant in the region, are generally brave fighters, very sincere and simple, and are one of the clans that also have the largest strength in the Nepalese Army, the Indian Gorkha regiments, and the British Gurkha brigades, the others being the Gurungs, Rais, and Limbus. In fact, they are, by general consensus, recognized as the perfect model of what a Gorkha soldier ought to be. Their other characteristic features are their short temper, their resilience, and the fact that most are uneducated. A high proportion of their population is concentrated in the mid-western districts where the Maoist movement commenced. 'The real Magars are divided into six tribes: Allea, Burhathoki, Gharti, Pun, Rana and Thapa.'[8]

It is an irony that despite years of free democratic exercise, Nepal still has the Brahmin caste that dominates virtually all sectors of statehood from politics to bureaucracy, journalism to judiciary, introducing a new nomenclature called *brahminbad*.[9] A substantial number of Chhetris and Newars are prominent in the police/ Army and the business sectors, but people of the lower castes have been totally marginalized in Nepalese society. 'Public policies that benefit particular communities, absence of minority heroes and symbols from [the] national pantheon, non-recognition of culture, customary laws and traditions, annexation of names and titles are other examples of cultural discrimination.'[10]

[8] Nagendra Kumar Singh, *Refugee to Ruler: Militant Races of Nepal*, New Delhi: APH Publishing, 1997, p. 56.

[9] The first politician publicly citing this political trend in the country was Ganesh Man Singh, who was criticizing the selection of ambassadors by the G.P. Koirala Government of his own party.

[10] Mahendra Lawoti, 'Defining Minorities in Nepal', *Nepali Journal of Contemporary Studies*, vol. II, no. 1, March 2002, p. 34.

Ethnic disharmony—a relatively new development in Nepal—has been bolstered by various sources over these 12 tumultuous years, although a faint call for the resurgence of the minorities had been heard during the Panchayati days as well. But an intense armed movement was impossible during the rule of a strong and effective leadership at the centre.

The change of 1990 aroused a new-found sense of identity and a legal ground for the *janjatis* to appeal for their demands. The dominating populace of the mid-west is famous for its feudal and supercilious nature, with the upper castes dominating and discriminating against the lower castes on the basis of religion, language, caste, and culture. Ethnic groups of the country have also been demanding reservations in different sectors. They claim that all their demands have always been brushed aside, and this demand for reservations is just one of them. *Janjati* leaders say that all they are asking for is to set aside a certain quota of jobs in the civil service, educational institutions, and even the legislature. By their estimates, though the *janjatis* form a major portion of Nepal's population, their representation in the civil service is a meagre 2.3 per cent. Dr Harkha Gurung, while elaborating on the quandary of the caste system, says that:

> the future of Nepalese society can be visualized by looking east, at the social dynamism of the Nepali speakers across the Mechi...(Who have)...charted the path of Nepali nationalism.... In contrast to Nepal, the politics of Sikkim and Darjeeling is not the monopoly of the upper castes.... The pillars of nationalism are social and economic integration....The most important step towards consolidating the Nepalese state and nationalism is to end economic exploitation and social injustice.[11]

The Maoists were quick to identify this opportunity and gave their class struggle an ethnic flavour. Ironically, the Maoist leadership is dominantly Brahmin, but the tactics worked in the mid-west, as Magars and *janjatis* supported the Maoists enthusiastically.

[11] Harkha Gurung, 'Nepal: Social Demography and Expressions', *New Era*, Kathmandu, 2001 (1st edn. 1998), p. 40.

Rightly speaking the focus should have been not purely on condemning the successes of one caste, but on getting to the bottom, to the marginalization of the lower social groups, without damaging the ethnic and religious harmony of the kingdom and jeopardizing national security, which had been intact since 1825 onwards. A strong, peaceful, Hindu kingdom that has enjoyed uninterrupted accord and harmony with other religious faiths such Buddhism, Islam, and Christianity has today fallen prey to the calls of those who regard the Hindu religion as having received disproportionate encouragement from the state and the King, who is himself a Hindu monarch. Hence, the call to turn Nepal from a Hindu kingdom into a secular state also holds ground, with almost all the major political parties, including the NC, the CPN(UML) and the CPN(Maoist), agreeing to this agenda. One is not sure, however, whether the proposed 'secular' designation of the country will pacify other religious faiths, or further antagonize the majority Hindus and set off a religious war as in India by polarizing various political groupings. (See Table A2.1, Annexure II for the *Janjati* Population.)

The Maoists have tried to establish links with the Khumbuwan Mukti Morcha (Khumbuwan Liberation Movement), which seeks to establish a separate state of specific castes. They have maintained that the *magurali* castes are not Hindus, which for years, perhaps centuries, 'they were forced to be'. They have, furthermore, started a campaign to stop celebrating the festival of *Dashain* [Dussehra], which, according to them, is the religious event of just the Hindus. The front was fighting for a state based on ethnicity mainly in east Nepal, and was involved in several incidents of murder and most recently in attacks on infrastructure.

> The Maoists who fled Solukhumbu and Okhaldhunga districts after the security forces intensified their activities there created havoc in Khotang. The villagers are caught between the crossfire from three sides—the Maoists, the security forces and the activists of the Khumbuwan *Mukti* Morcha in the south of the district.[12]

[12] 'Khotang's Plight', *Deshantar*, 27 January 2002, p. 4.

But as the Maoists are tired of using the long-standing disgruntlement of the *janjatis* and dalits [the downtrodden], primarily *sarkis*, *tharus*, and *damais* to the advantage of the people's movement, the Khumbuwan Mukti Morcha, on its part, has lately disassociated itself from the Maoists and disbanded the party. This development is definitely a setback to the Maoists.[13] Furthermore, Gore Bahadur Khapangi, an influential leader of the Morcha, joined the Chand Government and received the *Dashain tika* from the King, which was another setback to the whole movement for self-rule on the basis of ethnicity.

Janjati involvement in the movement has been a much-debated phenomenon, as there is no concrete evidence to support the argument(s), but most of it may well be true, as the prejudice of centuries may have created an ogre ready to devour anything.

DISSATISFACTION WITH THE JUDICIARY

After 1990, the Nepalese judiciary was formally separated from the executive and the legislature, and has also shown the resolve to be independent of any type of political influence, as evident from various landmark decisions. The judiciary has the right of judicial review under the Constitution, and the Supreme Court decides on major legal issues. HM the King appoints the chief justice and all other judges to the supreme, appellate, and district courts on the recommendation of the Judicial Council. All lower-court decisions, including acquittals, are subject to appeal. The Supreme Court has, through the interpretation of Art. 53(4) of the Constitution in the three cases of dissolution of the House, established a precedence of 'judge-made law', keeping itself above political-party influences.

There is no dearth of analysts who proclaim that the grime and dust prevalent in Nepalese politics is due to the Supreme Court verdict of reinstating a house dissolved by the King on the recommendation of the duly elected prime minister, thereby reducing the natural powers of the head of the government. On

[13] www. nepalnews.com, 28 May 2002.

the other hand, there are also complaints that justice is becoming too expensive and too slow, with many cases of corruption and rulings obtained through money. The judiciary is now overworked, with more than 35,000 civil cases pending in the courts, half of which are related to the division of the lower branches of the court itself. The number of cases filed in the courts is on the increase due to the lack of informal counselling centres that could unofficially resolve trivial family disputes, rather than taking the issues up to the judges who take years, even generations, to decide. One such classic case is of an 83-year-old lady, Safala Shrestha of Thamel in Kathmandu, made which headlines.[14] She has been knocking the doors of justice for the last 33 years. Senior judges, and lawyers at the Supreme Court all know her very well. She roams around different courtrooms in her quest for a share of the family's property. Perhaps the best explanation comes from Prakash Wasti, a senior lawyer, who says, 'We are still following court procedures adopted by Rana Prime Minister Jung Bahadur in 1853.'

Coupled with this are serious lapses in the implementation of the decisions of the Bench. It was reported recently that another woman was found to have spent five years in prison in addition to the jail sentence the court had given her. Such tragic examples are increasing and getting publicity, among the civil society and the rural folk.

It is probably due to this state of affairs that people in some of the remote districts have started to approach the *jana adalats* [people's courts] set up by the Maoists for justice. They have already replaced the government's courts in certain areas as the Maoist courts seem more fair, inexpensive, quick, and their decisions are executed very efficiently.

PRO-POOR APPROACH OF THE MAOISTS

Taking loans for one's family obligations, daughter's marriage, *Dashain* and *Deepawali* [Diwali] festivals, etc., is a common practice in rural Nepal. It is said that Nepalese peasants are born in debt,

[14] Keshav Poudel, 'Justice Delayed is Justice Denied: A Woman's Saga Tells how Pathetic the Situation of Nepalese Judiciary Is', *Spotlight* (Kathmandu), 26 January–1 February 2001, p. 20.

live their entire lives in debt, and leave behind a heavy debt for their children and grandchildren to pay back. Most of the time, pitiless village bourgeois landlords demand and keep on adding up astounding amounts as interest that keep adding up, forcing unfortunate farmers to become bonded labourers. Furthermore, large chunks of land are owned by a few property owners who customarily simply rent out their land for tilling. 'Atrocity' in a rural Nepali village is, therefore, commonly connected with the cruelty of the landlord(s). The Maoists knew this very well, and were not hesitant to cash in on this to the advantage of their activities. They cracked down forcefully on the local money-lenders, burnt 'I Owe You' notes in public, and even slaughtered some notorious bourgeois landlords. This in some ways enhanced the Robin Hood type image that the 'victimized' villagers had of the Maoists.

In order to be 'like little fishes in water' to the population, as Mao had directed, his Nepalese followers made it a point to punish not only the selfish landlords, but even rapists, village thugs and hooligans, and issue instructions to stop the sale of liquor (to get the sympathies of the rural womenfolk), banned all tobacco products, and prohibited all kinds of gambling at all times. They also encouraged the otherwise gullible Nepalese to end all superstitious practices: those not complying were punished severely. The mid-west region of Nepal does not have as many temples and monasteries as does the rest of the kingdom, and women-folk of particular castes are not constrained by the same religious dogmas prevalent among other castes. Women were encouraged to take up arms, give up the mundane chores of the household, and fight for equal rights. This came as a shock to the bucolic traditionalists, but what was more alarming was the deliberate intensification of the practice of cow slaughter. Being a Hindu kingdom with the cow as the national animal, cow slaughter is seen as equivalent to murdering a human, according to Nepalese law. However, it is also true that a section of the *janjatis* have had the custom of eating beef from time immemorial, a feature exploited by the rebels to rouse ethnic outbursts.

It also deserves mention that they, indeed, have erected a few martyr's gates in memory of their fallen comrades, constructed a small number of feeder roads, and attacked private schools to get the sympathy of the poor students studying at government schools without proper facilities and trained teachers.

A major reason for the women of the villages to get enticed by the works and beliefs of the Maoists was because of prohibition of alcohol, banning of gambling, and forbidding domestic violence. In certain areas, drunkards who used to beat their wives and spend most of their money on gambling were brought to the correct path after the start of the rebellion.

UNEMPLOYMENT

That 38 per cent of the Nepalese people are living below the poverty line is a big challenge to the policy-makers and a trial to the security forces, which see more and more young recruits to the Maoist insurgency. There is no doubt that the incidence of unemployment is largely responsible for giving rise to poverty. At present, 4.9 per cent of the people are unemployed, with the rate of semi-unemployment being as high as 47 per cent. A case in point: a record number of job-seekers applied for less than 600 posts of the Nepal Electricity Authority advertised recently. 'We expected up to 25,000 applications but more than three times as many applications turned up', says Ram Prasad Adhikari, personnel director of the utility authority. Altogether, the NEA had sold 120,000 application forms.[15]

Unemployment in the country is characterized by the following.

1. It is estimated that 300,000 labourers enter the market every year. But most of them are either unskilled or semi-skilled.
2. On the one hand, Nepalese labourers are facing unemployment, while on the other, migrant workers from the Indian states of Orissa, Bihar, and UP are displacing them.
3. The present condition of the economy has also painted a gloomy picture. Due to declining agricultural and industrial activities, the economic growth of the country stands at 0.8 per

[15] Ram Kumar Kamat, 'Too Many People, Fewer Jobs', *Rising Nepal*, 15 June 2002, p. 1.

cent, the lowest in the decade. Closure of factories, declining tourism, carpet, garment, and pashmina industries further add to the jobless.

4. One of the top sources of income for Nepal has, for long, been remittances from the Nepalese working abroad. More and more Nepalese are going abroad as security guards, helpers, construction labourers, etc. An increasing number of Nepalese girls are sold in brothels across India.
5. A substantial number go to neighbouring Indian towns for jobs. The mid-west region is primarily famous for the male population seasonally going to Indian cities to look for jobs.
6. Unemployment brings frustration, and that, in turn, begets anger against the state, a factor exploited by the Maoists.

Unless there is a concerted and serious action plan to address this disturbing trend, resolving the Maoist problem may be extremely difficult. The sad part is that as violence has increased, economic activity has seen a slowdown, resulting in losses to companies and the major sectors, thereby pushing up the unemployment ratio. Tourism being one of the biggest bread-earners of the country has seen a whopping slide partly due to the international publicity of Maoist violence and also because of misfortunes like the hijacking of IC-814, the royal massacre, and incessant Nepal *bandhs*. Major hotels in even big cities like Kathmandu and Pokhara are operating under big losses. Their smaller counterparts have had no option but to cut down on staff. And, consequently, the number of unemployed keeps increasing. As unemployment increases, more and more idle minds turn into Maoists' workshops.

Another important facet of the whole conundrum is the education system of the country, which, despite the millions spent by the government and donors, continues to be in a dismal condition. A considerable number of government school students do not even get through the school-level certificate examinations. A huge disparity exists between the privately-run schools and colleges and the corresponding government-owned ones. Even those who get through the high school ultimately choose the humanities fields of study and not science, IT, or commerce. Hence, technical manpower is invariably in short supply, while arts graduates cannot find good jobs.

MISHANDLING BY THE STATE

Although a 'democracy' (nicknamed demo*crazy*) is a never ending game of one-upmanship among politicians and political parties, it has encouraged variation in policies and programmes even when viewing urgent crises of statehood like the Maoist uprising. A tendency of being distinct from others in order to make a mark on the vote bank has resulted in political pandemonium. There is no consensus among major political blocs on any issue of national importance, be it foreign affairs, major economic policies, or even national security. Nepal does not even have a national security policy, for that matter, despite being a location of great geopolitical vulnerabilities, making it the only country on the earth which is sandwiched between two declared nuclear powers and in close proximity to another nuclear country. While political leaders tend to duplicate everything from the Indian political system, they have never learnt the foremost rule of the political culture that Indian politicians possess: need for having one voice on major national crises and standing up united on issues of national emergency. As a result, for the UML, the Maoist insurgency is 'a result of the gross abuse of authority by the Nepali Congress', for the NC it is 'a conspiracy of the extreme right and the extreme left to write off a central democratic force', and for the Rastriya Prajatantra Party (RPP) it is an 'obvious outcome of inexperienced political leadership'. Had there been an out-and-out rejection of Maoist ideology and its aggressive campaign from all sectors of the society from the time of its inception, probably the situation would have been different. There was, instead, and there still is, a large section of Kathmandu's elite including senior politicians, journalists, and academics who welcome the blow that the Maoists have been giving to the corrupt and crumbling state edifice. They actually appreciate the nationalistic stands of the Maoist leaders and feel that it is the dishonest and incompetent governments that came to power from 1990 onwards that are really to blame. The Maoists too have been quick to exploit this bitterness among the existing power blocs, and have used one against the other. They have never made the mistake of making either a verbal or armed offensive against all the power centres at the same time. The last time a famous leader committed this mistake was when Adolf Hitler attacked Soviet Russia when battles on other fronts were going on simultaneously. His fate is well-known to the Maoists.

At the very outset, the Nepali Congress government regarded the Maoist imbroglio as a law and order problem and left a politicized, disorganized, and ill-equipped police force to deal with the situation. The insurgents, who were already adept at exploiting all local seeds of conflict between progressive and traditional, between different religions, races, castes and clans, between local and foreign capitals, and between friendly national capitalists and anti-national bourgeois, had also been training and equipping their cadres in guerrilla warfare. Their political aim was to slowly gain control over the local, rural population, and the military aim was to offset the police, demoralize it and make it powerless. There was another important objective too—to capture the .303 rifles of the police and upgrade their strength force from the *khukri* (knife), and home-made gun.

At this point, it is essential to analyse the impact of the two major police actions undertaken by the Nepali police.

OPERATIONS ROMEO AND KILO SIERRA TWO

It is said that 'a conflict rises and escalates when two or more people or groups pursue goals that are mutually inconsistent'. For the intellectuals of selected areas of the mid-west, there was this ideological appeal of communism, which is why so many hundreds copies of Mao's Red Book and Maoist propaganda pamphlets had been so widely distributed. For the uneducated, there was this illusory allure of change from the status quo, hence even the tough training for guerrilla warfare was never looked upon as a hardship. Dreams are powerful weapons in themselves, and all one has to ensure is that they remain alive.

Nothing can be more appalling to innocent rural community than when a police battalion moves in, searching for insurgents. Because of the poor training of the police personnel and their lack of knowledge and proper orientation, instead of resolving the problem, they usually become a major problem themselves. This has happened often enough but it is still little understood.

In November 1995, the NC realized the dangers of the spread of extreme left groupings in the remote hills and decided to conduct Operation Romeo (Romeo for 'Rolpa'). This operation is regarded as having had a lasting impact on the minds of the people of Rolpa. As the police moved in, there were reports of rape, torture, and mass killings. Some even termed it 'a reign of terror'. The government ought to have been mindful of the fact that when force is used, there is always an outburst of anger against the state that even manages to antogonize those who have initially been unfriendly to the insurgents. But even as the whole operation was getting out of hand, there was no proper assessment of the campaign, no mechanism to precisely monitor the events on the ground, and no reward or punishment approach to the police personnel in action. In fact, only those officers who were not close to high-ranking brass were reported to be sent to the killing fields. According to local dwellers who have described their agony to the press, the police, in the wake of information regarding the insurgents' entry into a particular area, usually questioned a handful of local inhabitants and then went on a frenzy of searching and hunting the invisible enemy. Those who voluntarily or forcibly granted shelter to the Maoists were either killed, beaten, or arrested. Bewildered and confused, the villagers were in a tight spot between two armed, uncompromising diehards.

Baburam Bhattarai, while talking to *The Independent* in 1995, had a long story to tell regarding the operation.

> The situation in Rolpa is extremely tense and explosive at the moment. The present reactionary state managed by the three-party coalition of the Nepali Congress, the Rastriya Prajatantra Party (RPP) and the Sadbhawana Party, has launched the so-called Operation Romeo in the district since 4 November. Under this armed police operation around 1,500 policemen including a specially trained commando force sent from Kathmandu have

been deployed to let loose a reign of terror against the poor peasants of that rugged mountain district in western Nepal. So far about one thousand people have been arrested, of whom about three hundred are kept in police custody or sent to jails under fictitious charges while the rest have been released on bail or after severe torture. The people arrested range from 12 to 70 years of age and most of them have been subjected to inhuman torture while in police custody. An 18-year old girl from Gam VDC was raped in Sulichour police station; eight girls from Oowa VDC were stripped to nudity and tortured with *Sisnu Pani*. Numerous houses of poor peasants in Kotgaon VDC have been set ablaze and there has been indiscriminate ransacking and looting of properties of common people by the ruling party hoodlums under the protection of the police force. More than ten thousand rural youths, out of a population of two hundred thousand for the whole district, have been forced to flee their homes and take shelter in remote jungles. The armed police operation is still continuing and the virtual reign of white terror seems endless at the moment.

Even the official website of the Nepal Police records:

In order to tackle this [Maoist] problem in the initial phase, many reformative and psychological measures were adopted by HMG to bring them back on [the] right track and make them participate in the social service activities. Despite these reformative measures they plunged into the terrorist activities by staging attacks against innocent people of that locality. Later an operation code-named Operation Romeo was designed with a view to correct, educate and make them aware of their constitutional rights and obligations, which really didn't help and rather the situation worsened as they spearheaded to more killings.[16]

When the situation backfired due to the actions taken under Operation Romeo, another dreadful operation was undertaken in 18 districts known as Operation Kilo Sierra Two (radio code name for 'Search to Kill').[17] Within a year, the total number of the dead surpassed all previous records. The toll mounted on both sides as the saga of human rights violations escalated. Tragic footage and photos of killed insurgents and policemen with corpses being surrounded by wailing relatives began to flood the media and

[16] Nepal Police: www.nepalpolice.gov.np

[17] Deepak Thapa, 'Day of the Maoist', *Himal South Asia*, August 2000, p. 33.

were circulated around the world. Other armed police actions were also launched with various code names, specifically: Operation Kilo in Kalikot, Operation Juliet in Jumla, Operation Hotel in Humla, Operation Delta in Dolpa, and Operation Mike in Mugu districts of the Karnali zone. However, the intensity of the uprising was not alarming enough for these operations to take a severe turn.[18] Villagers still look back with anger at the thoughtless and rash police behaviour, while on an equally tragic note, the innocent family members of the deceased police personnel look back with melancholy at the many years of peace that the country had enjoyed in yesteryears. And the nation at large nurses the wounds of the follies that it committed in the name of nipping the insurgency in its bud.

In this case even the few local adversaries of the Maoists instantly turned against the government after operations Romeo and Kilo Sierra Two.

[18] It must be understood that Nepal was divided into 14 zones prior to 1990, after which they ceased to officially exist under the new Constitution, but the names of the zones are still widely used.

CHAPTER 4

Progress of the Rebellion

What started with a few diehard radical youths with *khukris* six years ago has today become a mighty rebellion of an unimaginable scale and a virtual alternate to the state. A record or in-depth analysis of the daily routine of Maoist activities from the time of its inception is not feasible for this monograph but it is important to record the attacks and looting from 1996 to 2000, and evaluate some of the major attacks and operations from the year 2000 onwards. The phase of late 2001 and early 2002 specially saw a terrific rise in the number of casualties. After the breakdown of talks between the government and the rebels in September 2003, a fresh round of violence commenced. The killing of an Army colonel in the heart of Kathmandu and assassination bids on a former state minister and another Army colonel terrified the capital city, resulting in massive security checks and night curfews.

As the movement now escalates into urban guerrilla warfare, its progress has moved very much on the lines chalked out by Mao Tse-tung. From strategic defence to strategic stalemate to strategic offence, the Maoists seem to be successfully following the course towards their objective. One can set apart the different phases of the armed revolt from the time of its inception, including the making of a base area, organizing terror, exploiting the law, and challenging a more powerful state security force, to the final phase of surrounding the cities. The three major phases of the progress of the insurgency are: the *khukri* phase, the .303 phase, and the automatic weapons phase. A brief summary of each phase is attempted in the following pages.

THE *KHUKRI* PHASE

The Maoist rebellion had a humble beginning, as the rebels were few, arms and ammunition were virtually non-existent, and training was close to nil.[1] Running a guerrilla organization is not easy as it has to possess practically everything—from food to water to arms and ammunition, from medicine to sports and music, and from uniforms to a sophisticated technological back-up of weaponry and communication. All these require money, but the only way to get resources are to loot the public or government (or both), or from donations and extortion. This, in turn, can only be successful after a brief reign of terror has been established and the movement gets publicity in the national and international media. The Maoists are known to be outstanding for their being publicity savvy all over the world, wherever the potential of a movement exists. Rolpa, Rukum, Gorkha, and Pyuthan were specifically chosen for the first attacks by novice mutineers who were inexperienced but fully aware of the ground reality of exploitation, massive anti-government feeling, feudal characteristics of the society, etc. Landlords who were unpopular in a particular village, aristocratic feudal lords well known for their cruelty and greed were purposely selected and either punished or killed with *khukris*. Killing someone with a gunshot and slashing him with a *khukri* are two very different acts of terror. Most of the time, the victim is only seriously hurt at the first slash of the knife, hence requires several slashes and chops. But it has enormous advantages for the assailant: it instils tremendous nerve, makes the spirit indomitable and fearless, and grooms him/her for tougher, more challenging pursuits in the future. Attacking village feudals has another facet: since most of them possess home-made guns, they can be looted and used during the insurgency. Entering villages in the darkness of night, wearing red headbands and chanting Maoist slogans, their other victims include local bureaucrats or government supporters. They are murdered by smashing their hands and legs with hammers and rocks. This, too, is a two-pronged strategy. First, it threatens other potential supporters of the police and the administration or informers; and second, it gives confi-

[1] One Maoist leader has even said that the movement started with just one .303 rifle.

dence to the attackers that if they can accomplish this with their hands or simply with a *khukri*, they can even defeat the state Army if they get automatic weapons.

On the very first day of the launching of the movement, the Maoists attacked Holeri police post in Rolpa (which was later re-erected). Telephone towers, electricity poles and roads were destroyed so as to thwart easy government mobility, and, additionally, to bring more villagers into the fold of the rebellion both by intimidation and appeal. On a sunny day in the middle of December 1997, a handful of Maoist rebels attacked Bethan police station in Ramechap district, which is thought to be the first major sensitive incident. Only *khukris* and one or two home-made guns were used. It caught the police completely off-guard. Until they had sufficient number of .303s looted from the Nepal police, and ammunition and training to use them, the guerrillas mainly used crude home-made weapons and gelignite bombs, which gave the impression to the power centres in Kathmandu that the insurgency was still at a nascent stage, with sufficient time to curtail it. There are several incidents where only the women cadres were used so as to bring in a level of buoyancy and confidence, while in other confrontations, the quantity of arms and ammunition looted augmented the arms and ammunition looted earlier from other police stations. Therefore, with the help of the *khukri* and home-made guns, if, for instance, the number of the .303s looted were 20, the number became three times higher with the use of those 20 rifles.

At about the same time, the freedom of the capital city Kathmandu and the international contact that it facilitates were utilized massively for publicity purposes. While police atrocities were the main target, intellectuals, well-known politicians and journalists were being impressed with the nationalistic posture assumed by the CPN(Maoist), since other ideological stands of the party did not have such an appeal for the city-dwellers. Here, the role played by the front organizations of the party is especially significant, and they made it a point to see that all these were active in their respective areas. Even the top leaders participated in some of their programmes to encourage, and cheer the activists. The author had met Baburam Bhattarai, Hisila Yami and Pampha Bhusal at the main gate of the Birendra International Convention Centre in Kathmandu just prior to the launch of the movement at a protest rally organized by the Akhil Nepal Mahila Sangh (Krantikari), a revolutionary women's association allied with the party. They were protesting against a 'Miss Nepal Contest' that, Ms Bhusal outlined, was an attempt to sell the flesh, the body, of young Nepalese girls for advertisement of products like beer.[2]

Even if people did not actively support the Maoist ideology, they may well be sympathetic to the demands of the 'All Nepal Meter Auto-Rickshaw Workers' Association' or the 'All Nepal Carpet Workers' Association'. A number of notable sister organizations that are functioning effectively and affiliated with the CPN(Maoist) are as follows.

1. Akhil Nepal Rashtriya Buddhijiwi Sangathan (All Nepal Intellectuals' Association).
2. Akhil Nepal Sikshak Sangathan (All Nepal Teachers' Association).
3. Akhil Nepal Swatantra Bidyarthi Union (All Nepal Free Students' Union).
4. Akhil Nepal Majdur Sangh (All Nepal Labour Union).
5. Akhil Nepal Painter Majdur Sangh (All Nepal Painters' Association).
6. Akhil Nepal Hotel and Restaurant Majdur Sangh (All Nepal Hotel and Restaurant Workers' Association).

THE .303 RIFLE PHASE

As the movement progressed, the cooperation sought from the Nepalese workers in India began yielding definite results. The mid-west has the maximum number of seasonal migrant workers who are employed in road and dam construction in India, which

[2] This writer was working at that time with the *Rising Nepal* daily. Dr Bhattarai said that he participated in the programme as the SJM supported the protest of the Akhil Nepal Mahila Sangh (Krantikari).

gives them access to stealing dynamite, detonators and fuses. At the same time, according to the anti-terrorist section of the Nepal police, the rebels started receiving supplies of electronic detonators and explosives with the capacity of destroying big installations and buildings from the People's War Group (PWG) of India, while the Maoist Communist Centre (MCC) made pistols, ammunition, and high-quality detonators available. The arms were usually brought into Kathmandu through the Terai and supplied to the mid-western districts. In 1999, a person carrying a huge consignment of detonators was arrested at Thankot check post, which serves as the main gateway to Kathmandu. The nature and quantum of arms that the rebels have is difficult to estimate, but according to the state security forces, they have mostly used the same weapons that were previously looted either from police stations or Army barracks. For instance, the Chinese-made pistols used in the assassination of Armed Police IG Krishna Mohan Shrestha and Col. Kiran Basnet in Kathmandu are the same ones used by the Nepal police officers on duty. Although a lot remains to be recovered (including sophisticated SMGs and LMGs), the RNA has organized a public display of recovered weaponry at Tundikhel. As money started pouring in, more sophisticated weapons such as AK-47s have also sneaked into rebel hands. In September 2003, Indian newspapers reported the seizure of a large cache of arms about to be purchased by the PWG and on its way to Nepal. Similarly, each operation has obviously been financed through the 'donations' of the rural folk, booty from the public sector banks, and extortions from business houses, including educational institutions in the cities.

Sporadic incidents were continued, as, during this stage, the rebels focused on gathering maximum cash from industrialists and businessmen in the main cities. With the prohibition campaign, a few distilleries were attacked, the major one being in Banke district. Private schools infamous for charging high fees were also attacked.

Speaking before the Parliament as early as July 1999, the then home minister disclosed that a total of 884 people had died, with more than Rs. 90 million worth of property lost in violent incidents since the inception of the Maoist movement:

> February 13th, 2000 marked the fourth anniversary of the start of the 'people's war.' As the anniversary was approaching, the Maoists have intensified their terrorist activities. On February 7th, the Maoists apprehended a bus in Dolakha district carrying 15 Polish tourists and six Nepalese guides and robbed them of about $5,000 in cash and personal belongings. Also on February 13th, the fourth anniversary, the chief commander Comrade Prachanda, issued a statement that his party may now be willing to negotiate with the government to end the violence, killings and abductions.[3]

While the Nepal government appeared to be mired in its own inefficiency and infighting within the ruling parties to prepare a comprehensive plan to face the Maoist challenge, 25 September 2000 turned out to be a major day in the history of the Maoist movement, as it changed the entire course of the rebellion. The 'People's Guerrilla Army' of the Maoists attacked government and police offices in Dunai Bazaar, the district headquarters of Dolpa district. They killed 14 policemen and left 40 policemen injured; 12 policemen guarding the local jail were reported missing. The office of the Chief District Officer (CDO), the district police headquarters, land revenue office, and several government-owned offices were also destroyed in the attack.

The guerrillas also destroyed the local jail with grenades, socket bombs and pipe bombs, freeing 17 prisoners. The only bank in the district, the branch of Nepal Bank Limited was captured by the guerrillas who looted Rs. 35 million in cash. What was remarkable about the assault was the proficiency shown by the guerrillas both in terms of warfare and intelligence gathering. Rs. 35 million had been deposited in that bank that very day. Although there have been unverified reports of bullets fired from automatic weapons in the attack, nothing substantial can be said in order to verify the report, hence, it was the maximum that the Maoists have accomplished with the help of the .303, which is an old, unsophisticated weapon that can fire only one shot at a time and needs to be reloaded after each firing.

[3] The Maoist Problem: www.nepal-school-projects.org/maoist%20problem.htm

An army barrack was situated nearby, but the rebels were clever enough to destroy a bridge connecting the barrack with the rest of the area prior to the attack. Even otherwise, they probably guessed that the army wouldn't come to aid the police until they received orders from the central high command. Although the government had approved four more districts, Dolakha, Dailekh, Surkhet, and Dang under the Integrated Security and Development Programme (ISDP) along with Kalikot, Gorkha, Rukum, Rolpa, Salyan, Pyuthan, and Jajarkot, the RNA (which had been deployed as per the objective of the ISDP) they did not have orders till then to confront the rebels.

THE AUTOMATIC WEAPONS PHASE

The lessons of Dunai were not heeded by the power centres of Kathmandu despite the shocking pictures of dead policemen and ruined government buildings with fires burning in the district headquarters shown on television even several days after the attack. Several other attacks around the kingdom followed the incident, with provocative articles in pro-Maoist newspapers and magazines of the guerrillas now being ready to counter an offensive of the army.

More was to come to add to the series of mishaps and ill-fated incidents to stun the Nepali populace. On 1 June 2001, the entire royal family was massacred by Crown Prince Dipendra. The incident could not have happened at a worse time, when the experience, sagacity, and maturity of King Birendra were needed, as he was looked up to with great respect and devotion by Nepalese and foreigners alike. While the devastating news shocked everyone, nobody in Kathmandu had seen a gathering quite as massive as the one of mourners that went along with the dead bodies of the late King and Queen to the cremation ghat at Pashupatinath. Thousands shaved their heads in reverence to the late monarch. The Maoists were quick to understand this public sentiment, and disclosed for the first time that they had a working relationship with the late King and respected him for his nationalistic stands. There were reports on BBC that some condolence books were also kept by the Maoists for their cadres to inscribe words of respect to the departed monarch. Baburam Bhattarai, in an article published in the vernacular *Kantipur* daily, wrote:

> King Birendra had been killed because he had stood up to the expansionary forces and against India. Similarly, King Birendra had been the one who was unwilling to have the Army deployed to fight the 'people's war'. There had been a similarity in approach between the late King and the Maoists.[4]

The rebels and the newly-formed Deuba Government announced a ceasefire following the resignation of the government of Girija Prasad Koirala which succumbed to a sequence of corruption cases, Maoist attacks, and demands for resignation by the opposition. Koirala announced his resignation on state radio and TV, saying the country was 'passing through a very serious situation' because of attacks by Maoist rebels. 'If all political parties do not confront the crisis united, the country will face an even graver situation in the future', he said.

Just before his resignation, on 12 July 2001, about 1,500 insurgents attacked a police post in Holeri in Rolpa taking 71 policemen hostage. The RNA had gone into action against Maoist rebels in the hills of western Nepal, surrounding hundreds of rebels in their hideout in Nuwa village of that district. 'The army action came as troops began searching for [those] policemen who were abducted by Maoist guerrillas on a raid at the Holeri police post.' Army officials in Kathmandu said that the rebels, triggering a gun battle, fired upon an RNA helicopter ferrying troops to the site.[5] There were conflicting reports from the army and the rebels as both used propaganda warfare to bluff the other. But after the formation of the Deuba Government, there was, suddenly, a positive turn of events with the release of 33 hard core Maoist prisoners. A series of peaceful negotiations started, which will be analysed in the following chapter.

[4] The editor and the publisher of *Kantipur* daily were detained by the administration for printing this article.

[5] *Kathmandu Post*, 14 July 2001, p. 1.

The cushion of time offered by peaceful negotiations has frequently been exploited by guerrillas to regroup, re-equip, and plan ahead. The PWG in Andhra Pradesh suddenly broke off from the talks with the government of Chief Minister Chandrababu Naidu and afterwards managed to trap a handful of commandos—a clear demonstration that they had emerged stronger. Elsewhere too, they tend to manipulate the favourable atmosphere to their advantage with the freedom of movement and speech. While the ceasefire was still on, the Maoists planned a mass rally in Kathmandu, and to the dismay of the rather pampered citizens of the capital city, began asking for accommodation and food for the cadres who were coming in from the far corners of the country. They managed to hold one rally at Basantapur, in the heart of the city. The terrified administration reminded them that mass rallies and confrontational situations only obstructed the way towards peaceful resolution of problems. 'Prime Minister Sher Bahadur Deuba [furthermore] appealed to the Maoists to stop violent terrorist acts and to follow the government-declared ceasefire. He specifically asked the Maoists to immediately stop extortion and cease holding mass meets with armed cadres around.'[6] Comrade Prachanda said on 22 November 2001, 'Since our demand for a Constituent Assembly has been ignored by the government, we have ascertained that the peace negotiation with it is fruitless.' He also struck an ominous note, saying that the latest developments (of the government disagreeing with the demand for a Constituent Assembly) 'makes the cease-fire meaningless'.

Whether this was born out of realization of the futility of the talks or due to pressure from the cadres is uncertain, as, on 11 August, five sister organizations of the party had issued a statement saying that they would raise weapons against their leaders if the establishment of a people's republic was not placed on the agenda. With this background, the talks that were going on were meant for publicity, and the ceasefire was beyond doubt heading towards a breakdown. In a statement issued on 21 November, Prachanda said, 'Now there is no alternate before the Nepalese

[6] *Kathmandu Post*, 25 August 2001, p. 1.

people other than to continue their struggle for nationalism, democracy and livelihood.'

On the very first day after breaking the truce, the People's Liberation Army attacked Syangja and Dang district headquarters. In Ghorahi, the district headquarters of Dang (the office of the district administration), the armed police district headquarters, the RNA barrack, district jail, banks, land revenue office, tax and forest offices were completely destroyed. During the attack, 14 soldiers (including the commander of the barrack) were also killed; 37 prisoners were freed after a jailbreak. Hundreds of modern weapons, including SLRs [self-loading rifles], SMGs [Sten machine guns/carbines], LMGs [light machine guns], light pistols, mortar grenades, hand grenades, and several thousand rounds of ammunition were captured.

In Syangja too, 14 policemen were killed and 34 prisoners freed. More than 150 rifles and about Rs. 200 million in cash were seized from the local bank. On 25 November, the rebels simultaneously attacked the CDO office, army barrack, and two banks in Solukhumbu district. There were 34 confirmed casualties on the government side. The government promptly declared a state of emergency, termed the Maoists as 'terrorists', and that those found involved, directly or indirectly, of helping them, would also be treated as terrorists.

With this gradual intensification of violent actions, one can easily get the drift of the movement from the stage of a humble *khukri* to the capacity of rendering an entire army barrack helpless in front of a swarming crowd of not only rebels, but also of women, children, and naive peasants. From the attack in a mud house of a 'bourgeois landlord' in Rolpa to the deadly assault in Dang's military barrack, the rebels have naturally gained a lot of strength (moral, financial, and technical) from a lot of people, and a spur to forge ahead. Training and coordination with proper communication resulted in the mayhem at Dang barrack, coupled with the confusion and mismanagement that gripped the army personnel. But it did one thing constructive: the army was now openly in the fray, and with a rich history of bravery and heroism in war, it had to prove itself up to the mark.

ARMY INVOLVEMENT

Demoralization, politicization, and erosion of the image of an otherwise effective police force under various governments over the last decade had sent wrong signals to the palace, which suspected that the RNA too might face the same fate if it was sent to solve a messy tangle emanating from the disillusionment of the previous 12 years. The army is perhaps the principal actor in major conflicts such as this, but mostly it is neither the creator nor the principal authority in bringing about a final resolution of the problem(s). Sadly, Nepal does not have a history of debate, discussion, and analysis pertaining to safeguarding national security with a view to eliciting public support so crucial for any successful army operation. Efforts should have been geared towards ensuring a proper balance between the military and civil effort with appropriate coordination in all fields. The RNA soldiers have definitely received suitable training and possess the backing of a better armoury, but insurgencies, and specially jungle warfare, are always difficult to outmanoeuvre, particularly without a higher sense of national interest at the level of the common man and the sincerity of political masters.

Furthermore, the army in Nepal has always remained insulated from the civilian society. As a result, a myth was created that if it came to battle, any problem would be resolved in a matter of weeks, if not days. As it remained confined to its quarters, it probably never regarded good press relations as being a vital factor in counter-insurgency. But the image of the army ran into problems in Dang, and then in Syangja, Rukumkot, Naumule, Holeri, Salleri, and Mangalsen. The Maoists were swift in boasting of their newly-found credentials. The Maoist magazine *Janadisha* stated:

> the opening horizon of the red future where we the oppressed will be the owner of our country not the slave of the corrupt politicians and feudal is visible. The emergency is training very well millions of people who didn't have the chance to fight in the battlefield.

Ironically, it wasn't the corrupt politicians or the feudals of Kathmandu who were killed by their brutal offensive, but the poor policemen, soldiers, or the innocent public in the area. But in strictly military terms, the army didn't seem geared for the offensive; even the then Chief of Army Staff accepted that the soldiers inside the Dang barrack were taken completely by surprise.[7] Over time, the men in green were getting experienced with the terrain (the 'ground reality', as they call it), when another armed action on 17 February 2002 by the Maoists came as a big blow not only to the army but to the entire state structure. This time they fought with sophisticated automatic weapons and rocket launchers looted from the Dang barrack.

The news report from a daily tells the poignant tale of the horrors witnessed at Mangalsen in Achham district.

Even hours after the eight-hour-long mayhem beginning at midnight at Mangalsen, fire was seen leaping from the destroyed buildings that were blasted by thousands of Maoists. The scene, coupled with the largest number of casualty (*sic*) on the government side so far, was a testimony that Maoists had perpetrated their most audacious attack since the start of their 'People's War' six years ago. The attacks at Mangalsen, the district headquarters of Achham, and at Sanfebagar, were undertaken simultaneously. Only one of the 58-man-strong army contingent in the army barracks survived the attack, but with injuries. The other 57, were all charred, and unrecognizable. On the other hand, the gunfight at Sanfebagar between the police and the Maoists lasted five hours. Both the areas surrounding Mangalsen and Sanfebagar are bathed in blood, which indicates that the Maoists too have suffered a heavy loss in the bloody battle.[8]

The Asian Age reported that the explosives used in the recent Maoist attacks might have been stolen from the collieries of Burdwan and Asansol districts of West Bengal. The report said that the Maoists must have received these explosives from the PWG and the Maoist Coordination Centre, based in Andhra Pradesh and Bihar respectively. The Indian police said these two extremist forces had stolen hundreds of detonators and explosives

[7] Gen. Prajjwolla S.J.B. Rana said this in an interview to Vijaya Kumar Pandey of Nepal Television.

[8] Manmohan Swarn, *Kathmandu Post*, 18 February 2002, p. 1.

over the years. 'We cannot yet say for sure, but what is certain is that Maoist rebels did steal detonators from Burdwan district', Superintendent of Police B.N. Ramesh was quoted as saying in Kolkata. But after Mangalsen, the Maoists have not been able to make such a strike on an army barrack.

Here, it is worthwhile to assess—through the little information that is available—the structure and strength of both the state army and the Maoists.

ORGANIZATION OF THE ROYAL NEPAL ARMY

The strength of the RNA is about 60,000. His Majesty the King of Nepal is the Supreme Commander-in-Chief of the Royal Nepalese army. The Chief of the Army Staff (COAS), a four-star general, is responsible for looking after the regular affairs of the Army. Recently, two posts of lieutenant generals have been created, Chief of the General Staff (CGS), and Chief of Staff (COS). The CGS is mainly responsible for the Operations, Intelligence and Training branches. A brigadier general heads each of these three branches. The Directorate of Military Operations (DMO) is responsible for operations, planning, policy, staff duties, budget requisition and allocation, and public relations. Similarly, the Directorate of Military Intelligence (DMI) and the Directorate of Military Training (DMT) are responsible for intelligence and training respectively. The COS is responsible for operations other than warlike UN Peacekeeping operations, Nature Conservation and Wildlife Preserve operations, National Cadet Corps, and various welfare schemes of the army.

The Adjutant General (AG), the Quarter Master General (QMG), the Master General of Ordnance (MGO) and the Inspector General (IG), all two-star generals, are the other principal staff officers of the COAS.

The RNA is organized into combat brigades, combat support brigades, and combat service support brigades. Each combat brigade is responsible for a particular area and is augmented with necessary combat support and combat service support elements. One of the combat brigades is designated a Royal Guards Brigade, and there is also a Special Forces Brigade.

A combat brigade is commanded by a brigadier general and comprises infantry battalions and independent infantry companies. Depending upon the geographical region, each combat brigade may have two to three infantry battalions and up to six or more independent infantry companies. A signal company, an engineer field company, a light artillery battery, an air defence battery, a field ambulance company, transport elements, ordnance elements, and workshop elements augment each combat brigade.

An infantry battalion, commanded by a lieutenant colonel, comprises rifle companies, a support company, and an administrative company. Majors command companies and lieutenants command platoons. Captains are the company seconds-in-command, and *jemadars* (junior commissioned officers) are the seconds-in-command of the platoons. A platoon consists of three sections, each section being commanded by a *hudda* (sergeant), a non-commissioned officer.

The support company of an infantry battalion consists of a mortar platoon, a medium machine gun platoon, an anti-tank platoon, signal platoon, and an assault pioneer platoon. A captain commands each of these platoons and *subedars* are their seconds-in-command.

Brigadier generals command all the support brigades. Field Artillery, Air Defence Artillery, Engineers, and Signals have their own brigades. Each brigade is responsible for the training, posting, and promotion of the other ranks. Each brigade commander is also responsible to advise the COAS on matters pertaining to his respective arm.

Similar to the combat support brigades, the combat service support brigades are also commanded by brigadier generals. Similarly, the brigade commanders are their respective services advisers.[9]

After imposition of the state of emergency and the promulgation of the ordinance relating to internal security, there has been better coordination between the related security agencies of the state, mainly the army, police, and the armed police.

A vital area of any counter-insurgency operation is the work of

[9] RNA HQ: www.rna.mil.np

the intelligence agencies. Nepal has altogether three intelligence services: the Rastriya Anusandhan Bibhag under the Home Ministry, one of the Nepal Police, and the DMI under the RNA. During the Panchayat days, a separate Royal Bureau of Investigation used to operate with a head office inside the palace, which has been disbanded after 1990. Intelligence agencies all over the world function in secrecy and one does not (or is not) entitled to know what they are doing. But in the Nepalese context, they have been so protected that there has never been a debate on the effectiveness of the intelligence bureaus, their information gathering and early warning capacities, and ability to penetrate any political group whether during the 30 years of Panchayat rule or in the multiparty era. Moreover, politicians (mainly the successive home ministers in the post-1990 era) have found a comfortable avenue to employ the idle young voters of their respective constituencies in the Rastriya Anusandhan Bibhag, which has resulted in deterioration of the quality and reliability of the agency. The intelligence agency of the Nepal Police is regarded to be far better equipped both in logistics and quality manpower. Fortunately, the jealousy and mistrust among the three units ended after November 2001, and they are now working together cooperatively against the Maoist rebels.

The whole debate of the need to bring the RNA under civilian or parliamentary control stems from the *de facto* (not *de jure*) control of the organization by the palace, which historically emanates from the time of the unification of the country in the early nineteenth century. His Majesty is the Supreme Commander-in-Chief of the RNA, but so are the President of India, the King of Thailand, or the Queen of England Supreme Cs-in-C of their respective armies, for that matter. In purely legal terms, the Constitution of the Kingdom of Nepal has provisioned the Royal Nepal Army to be under a National Security Council (NSC) to be headed by the Prime Minister, with the Defence Minister and the Chief of the Army Staff as members. Not understanding the pre-eminence of a civilian majority in the NSC in vital decision-making of the Army, which, as per the formation of the NSC, should originate from the elected prime minister, arguments to put the RNA under the Parliament have been increasing. What is puzzling to examine or even baffling to predict is how the swift decision-making of the army can be maintained in the case of 265 MPs getting the feeling that they are heading an institution as sensitive as the army. A better rapport between the palace and the government would have ensured that this unnecessary confusion on the use of the army was never created, but here too one can sense the brilliant strategic planning and the nicety with which it has been carried out by the Maoists. Till the royal massacre, they were vying on the 'nationalistic agenda', thereby signalling to the palace that they were for an alliance to defeat the anti-national elements (read the NC). However, in the post-massacre scenario, they have been increasingly prone to cash in on the 'full democracy' slogan, thereby indicating to the political parties that democratic forces should unite and forge an alliance against the palace. Both the palace and the parties have clearly fallen prey to this trap, which has hindered joint collaboration of all the major constitutional forces in the country against the Maoists. This has obviously placed the RNA in a difficult predicament, but it must not be suspected that it is merely a ceremonial army incapable of carrying out vital responsibilities when the state and its people have demanded determined and unwavering action from their army. The Khampa episode was one such case when the RNA exhibited its training and resoluteness in implementing the given tasks. Even with changing times, the army is still one of the most prestigious professions in Nepal, with the best and the brightest youngsters each year vying to get recruited. It has been a tradition that one son of almost every affluent family from the Thakuri clan gets into the army. But it is not that other castes and social groups don't excel in the RNA. There have been many such stories of success: today, more generals in the RNA are non-Ranas or non-Shahs.

ORGANIZATION OF THE MAOISTS

On the eve of voting on ratification of the state of emergency, the parliamentary State Affairs Committee (SAC) raised a question on the efficiency and performance of the RNA since its mobilization.

The SAC asked Prime Minister Sher Bahadur Deuba to take immediate measures to improve the army's level of performance. Their anxiety emanated from reports that the army had not been able to penetrate into the hinterlands of the rebels, but subsequent to the Mangalsen attack, their performance has improved considerably.

The Maoist organization structure is depicted in Fig. 4.1.[10]

	Politburo →	Central Military Commission	
	Central Committee	↓↓↓	
Open Organizations→	Regional Bureaus	Company→	Brigade
	Subregional Bureaus	Platoon	
	District Committee	Squad	
	Sector Committees	*Jan* [People's] Militia	
	Preliminary Sector Committees	Security Force	

Fig. 4.1 Stages of Maoist Organization

They have divided the country geographically into three zones and 27 districts, although their planning, organization, and tactics keep changing. The areas to the east of Sindhuli and Makwanpur and some parts of Lalitpur fall in the Eastern Zone. This zone is under the command of Yam Prasad Gautam alias Alok; Sub-Zone I of the Eastern Zone is under the command of Agni Sapkota; Sub-Zone II is under the control of Chitra Narayan Shrestha. The Central Zone includes districts from Rapti and Gandaki regions, which used to be commanded by Dr Baburam Bhattarai himself, Sub-Zones I and II being controlled by Shashi Shrestha and Hisila Yami. The Western Zone spreads in the districts from Rapti, Bheri, Karali, Sethi-Mahakali and Gandaki regions. This is under the control of Krishna Bahadur Mahara. Sub-Zones I and II are under Man Bahadur Mahara and Santosh Bura respectively.[11]

[10] This is only a hypothetical diagram based on widely published reports.

[11] Anju Susan Alex, 'Maoists of Nepal': www.ipcs.org

Although the impact of mobilization of the security forces on the rebels is only a presumption, some clearly noticeable features can be listed. We will conduct both forms of scrutiny, first with the view that the state security has been successful, and the second that there is still a long way to go.

ARGUMENTS THAT THE SITUATION IS COMING UNDER CONTROL

1. While the army has deposited looted money recovered from the rebels into the Nepal National Bank, there have been televised reports of some relatives of senior Maoist leaders depositing robbed public money into their private accounts.
2. On 6 June 2002, the army demonstrated a large quantity of weapons, photographs, explosives, money and other goods confiscated from the Maoist terrorists. The arms included: twenty-nine 7.62 mm SLRs with 233 magazines and 24 bayonets; three 9 mm SMGs with 81 magazines and 6 bayonets; and five 7.62 mm LMGs with 237 magazines. Among the ammunition were twenty-six 81 mm mortar smoke bombs, eleven 2-inch mortar HE bombs, etc.
3. The Maoists have attacked bridges, hydropower projects, water supplies, telecommunication towers, schools, and irrigation canals, inviting massive public criticism and also proving correct the analysis that they may now be getting desperate. Also, with school children getting killed, public sympathy may be waning.
4. A few area commanders have been killed during the operations. The rebels have not been able to deliver a solid strike after the Achham attack.
5. A broad understanding with both India and China, assistance from donor countries (primarily the US) has helped in cornering the Maoists internationally. More helicopters, modern arms, and logistic support coupled with additional government budget have definitely strengthened the security forces.
6. The Maoists have not succeeded in making any major attack on any military barrack lately and have instead concentrated

on assassinations, minor blasts in the capital and elsewhere, and setting up booby traps on highways.

ARGUMENTS THAT THE SITUATION HAS NOT COME UNDER CONTROL

1. Not even a single prominent Maoist leader has been killed or arrested.
2. Large tracts of territory in Rukum, Rolpa, Jajarkot, Salyan, Kalikot, and other districts are still under rebel control. The security forces have not been able to find their hideouts and training places, let alone flushing them out. Their communication network still seems to be intact.
3. Instead of yielding, the rebels are making inroads into other districts, specially in the Terai and the eastern zones of the kingdom.
4. They seem largely united; their military and ideological blocs don't appear to be at loggerheads despite lots of publicity about it.
5. Recruitment of the cadres is still going on. Governments keep getting formed and dismissed in Kathmandu on the issue of law and order situation.

During the Dang and Achham attacks, the insurgents used thousands of innocent civilians as cover. Consequently, the majority of those killed by the army were civilian, and not hard-core guerrillas.

It is a hypothesis that despite much effort by the security forces, recruitment by the rebels may still be going on unobstructed, and ample proof exists in this regard.

In any insurgency, there are four major types of recruits: (a) the naturals (b) the converted (c) the deceived and (d) the beleaguered.

It has widely been felt that massive recruitment is going on and the attacks on the army barracks and one armed police barracks are testimony to this, where a large number of innocent villagers were used by the rebels both as human shields and as forcible entrants. Without the government being alert and sincere on the

Legality + construction + results = government
Illegality + destruction + promises = insurgents

Fig. 4.2 Divergence Between Insurgents and Governments

larger grievances of the people like corruption, price-rise, lack of drinking water, sanitation, education, roads, etc., even if the Maoist movement is crushed militarily, there is likelihood of another deadly conflict stemming from the massive sense of frustration amongst the Nepalese rural folks. Sir Robert Thomson has formulated an equation (Fig. 4.2) to distinguish between the insurgents and the government, probably hinting at the way to go for a permanent solution to any insurgency.

CHAPTER 5

Defeating Communist Insurgency

Countering insurgency is not an easy proposition and as the world witnesses more and more armed rebellions, managing and controlling the situations arising from mass uprisings becomes a challange for the security forces. Growing recourse to guerrilla warfare has produced greater sophistication of guerrilla techniques. Most of the time, it is the politicians, who create the problems or indeed exacerbate them and it is the security forces who are called in to control the situation. The army in most cases is neither the creator nor the ultimate settler of the dispute.[1] And it is not the politicians but the security forces that face the criticism for the deteriorating law and order situation. When the Maoist guerrillas attacked private schools, parliamentarians criticized the home ministry and not the education policy pursued and implemented by the education ministry which resulted in the total neglect of the government-run schools. Hence, preventive detention, early warning, conflict resolution, countering guerrilla warfare effectively, and formulating war strategies best suited for countering an enemy who uses hit and run tactics need to be an essential part of every soldier's training.

Two case studies of Malaya and South Vietnam serve as apt barometers of how, and how *not*, to try and defuse an armed communist uprising. In Malaya, the communist insurgency was totally crushed (with the help of the Gorkha forces); in South Vietnam, the communist guerrilla forces defeated the large-scale

[1] Erstwhile Chief of Army Staff Gen. Prajjwolla S.J.B. Rana said in an interview to Vijaya Kumar Pandey that ultimately there would have to be peaceful negotiations to resolve the problem, and the army's role was only to make sure that the government negotiated from a point of strength.

conventional army backed by the Americans, spearheaded by over 1,20,000 North Vietnamese troops, crossed the demilitarized zone in the central highlands and took over the capital, Saigon. Despite President Nixon's response, 'The bastards have never been bombed like they are going to be bombed this time', there was nothing that could stop the Viet Cong despite 5,25,000 men, billions of dollars, and extensive bombing that the Americans unleashed on them.[2] The information and tactical measures adopted by military strategists to overcome the situation of hostility which will be of use as Nepal tries to manage the insurgency at the moment is listed below.[3] The paradox of the two situations is clearly visible.

1. In Malaya, there were basically two government forces: the police, and the army. In South Vietnam, there were the Armed Forces, the Civil Guard, the Self-Defence Corps, the Gendarmerie, the National Police, the Self-Defence Forces, the Republican Youth, Hamlet Militia, and the Women's Solidarity Movement.
2. Malaya had the advantage of having its northern border with Thailand, with which there was a border agreement under which the Malayan police could operate across the border. South Vietnam did not enjoy this advantage.
3. Malaya had a sound administrative structure, a strong, independent and respected judiciary, and a government that regarded the economic well-being of the country as its primary goal. There were unwritten but well-understood rules of the game. In South Vietnam, on the contrary, the Constitution was abrogated after the fall of President Diem, leading to a state of continuous instability: the focus was on building the military prowess, the country possessed a very large and corrupt ad-

[2] Larry Berman, 'Vietnam War', in *Encyclopedia of US Foreign Relations*, ed. Bruce W. Jentleson and Thomas G. Paterson, New York: Oxford University Press, 1997, p.269.

[3] Based on Robert Thomson, *Defeating Communist Insurgency*, New York: Friedrich A. Praeger, 1966; John J. McCuen, *The Art of Counter-Revolutionary War*, London: Faber and Faber, 1966, p. 33; and Brig. C. Aubrey Dixon and Otto Heilbrunn, *Communist Guerrilla Warfare*, Friedrich A. Praeger, 1962, p. 56

ministration, and too many people influencing government decision-making.

4. In Malaya, the government used the media to 'persuade' not just 'inform' the people that if the communists took over, ethnic Chinese would be the rulers. To be persuaded, people needed first to believe and trust the newspapers—an important aspect of counter-insurgency to which the government always gave importance. In South Vietnam, psychological warfare was to the advantage of the communists, not the government. Even with four major spoken languages Malaya had just 10 daily newspapers. Till the fall of Saigon, South Vietnam was well into producing more than a hundred dailies which survived on rumours and third-rate gossip and depended on blackmail for their income.

With these distinct dissimilarities, experts have framed methods for effective counter-insurgency campaigns based on their experience in Malaya and South Vietnam.

1. The government must have a clear political aim: to establish and maintain a free, independent, and united country which is politically and economically stable and viable.
2. The government must function in accordance with the law. Even dreaded terrorists must be tried freely in court. This brings about a sense of trust in the different organs of the state.
3. The government must have an overall plan, operational and logistical, including political, social, economic, administrative, police, and other measures which have a bearing on the insurgency.
4. The government must give priority to defeating political subversion, not the guerrillas. Its focus must be on educating the people about the absurdity of the ideology embraced by the rebels, not defaming their leaders.
5. Government forces must secure the base areas of the guerrillas first. This has tremendous psychological impact not only on the insurgents, but more so on the general population.
6 The main strategy of the rebels is to become to the population like little fish in water. The aim of counter-insurgency, there-

fore, should be to take these fish out of the water. All policemen and soldiers must be educated that the sole concept behind successful anti-communist operations is the physical and political separation of the guerrillas from the population.

7. The chief emphasis should be on clear-and-hold operations rather than on search-and-clear. Short-term raids in the war zones, achieve no lasting results. A sustained and enduring operation, draining the morale and supply of the guerrillas, is far more successful.
8. A favourite tactic adopted by the Viet Cong was of ambushing military convoys. But the guerrillas could prove to be equally vulnerable, if only movements of their forces, supplies, couriers, agents, etc., could be similarly known. In Malaya, most successful ambushes were carried out by groups of two to five soldiers at night.
9. In an insurgency, it is not major operations that defeat the insurgents, rather it is the high rate of contact in minor operations. In South Vietnam, the average was as bad as one contact to every 150 operations. Therefore, emphasis should be on effective intelligence mechanisms,resulting in more frequent and rapid contacts.
10. Japan had only eight national dailies and Malaya four. Gossip and smear campaigns by newspapers must be stopped, but censorship tends to make the government unpopular, hence creates disbelief even when successes are gained by the forces.
11. Three indispensable qualities in countering insurgency are patience, determination, and an offensive spirit. The last should be tempered with discretion, steady pressure, and a methodological approach to wear the insurgents down.

The counter-operations conducted by the RNA have not, of course, been fault-free, but one needs to also accept that there was over-expectancy that it would bring the situation back under control within weeks, if not days. Such high hopes usually tend to make the army take hasty measures to prove its might. After the disaster at Dang, where the barrack was totally overrun after the soldiers were caught by surprise, in Holeri, which was really the first encounter between the rebels and the army, the situation could have been better. But, as reported by the newspapers, a few rebel leaders managed to escape the army cordon. The tragedy in Achham could clearly have been avoided, as it was reported that the chief district officer had even telephoned Kathmandu and warned of a massive Maoist attack a good three days earlier. In Gam of Rolpa, despite the terrain, the army managed its first offensive. It wasn't as successful as initially expected, but one thing became clear: the soldiers were getting used to the topography and the circumstances, which are vital for any force accustomed only to celebrations and peacekeeping missions. Barring one single incident of the Khampas, which, too, is 28 years old this is what they were primarily engaged with. But as mentioned by Thomson and other writers, slow but sustained operations with few casualties, but which constantly deplete the ammunition, food, medicine, and logistics supply of the rebels, and finally alienate them from the population is what makes these operations successful. This would take more time than the cocktail circuit of Kathmandu would want, perhaps.

Similarly, counter-revolutionary warfare often requires local actions, and the officials at the grass-roots level need to rebuild that vital 'human contact' with the local population. The French used a massive civil training programme during the Algerian struggle and encouraged promising local leaders and youths to return. Administrative vacuums continue to encourage revolutionary movements, therefore, the need for a combined effort of all the sections of the population to back the efforts of the security forces needs to be emphasized. It has been seen that political parties are good only at criticizing, not at mobilizing their cadres against insurgency. Their leaders almost never visit the Maoist-prone areas to conduct public awareness campaigns. Instead of calling for *bandhs* in Kathmandu, they could go with the security forces and boost the morale of the public. The civil society, artists, and musicians too could hold programmes to encourage the security personnel. These, sadly, are what Nepal lacks.

As military operations escalate, the defence budget tends to scale up without check by any quarter. For the first time in history, the annual budget of Nepal has put its regular expenditure more than the development expenditure, owing to a massive increase of the expenses of not only the army, but also the police, the armed police, and the intelligence service. As in scenes of armed clashes elsewhere in the world, in Nepal too, there is imminent danger of the birth of a new class of people luridly called 'conflict entrepreneurs' who have vested interests in sustaining the conflict and not in resolving it. As stories of lucrative arms deals make headlines, it is doubtful whether the political masters or their subordinates in uniform, will want to settle the issue when easy money flows to them as a result. In such cases, one disaster gives birth to another, as illustrated in Fig. 5.1.

Armed uprising
$\downarrow\uparrow$
Political instability
$\downarrow\uparrow$
Need for more weapons
$\downarrow\uparrow$
Corruption/lucrative financial dealings

Fig. 5.1: The Viciousness of Insurgency

There has been much comparison between Peru's Shining Path and the Nepalese Maoists. According to Stephen L. Mikesell, a research scholar writing for *Himal* magazine:

> appealing geo-cultural analogies can be drawn between Peru and Nepal. Both countries straddle major mountain ranges of their respective continents, in which isolated valleys and high ridges have given way to a wide variety of cultural traditions. While neither country has a history of a recent foreign military conquest and occupation, as was the case in China in the 1930s, both have large rural indigenous populations subordinated to small ruling elites whom they divided by racism or casteism and regionalism.

The activists of the Shining Path were gunned down in Peru and its leader Comrade Gonzalo arrested—probably an encouragement to the government to crush the uprising the way the Fujimori Government tried to do in Peru. If Nepal wishes to learn from the counter-insurgency operations conducted successfully across Malaya, there would be a string of incidents to learn from. In addition, the El Salvador model could be studied to advantage. In El Salvador, both sides agreed to hold negotiations because there was: (1) a stalemate and neither side could win; (2) increasing public clamour for peace; (3) willingness of the UN to help out; and (4) withdrawal of support from neighbouring Nicaragua and Cuba. Ultimately, a negotiated compromise package was worked upon.[4]

In Peru, on the other hand, the Shining Path launched its movement the very day the first democratic elections were held in the country after 17 years. It was never willing to negotiate. The government launched a massive pro-poor programme in the rural countryside where the Shining Path had penetrated. Fortunately, the extreme poverty was reduced in the period 1993–8 from 31 to 15 per cent. In addition, its independent intelligence agency was successful in arresting Comrade Gonzalo when he was without bodyguards and completely alone. This is how counter-insurgency operations were conducted in Peru.[5] Unfortunately, Nepal has been trying a mix of peaceful negotiations and military operations, but without sufficient homework and without garnering the support of the people, resulting in a confused response that has only helped the rebels. A clear-headed approach either on talks across the table, or security mobilization in the hills and fields may perhaps yield sustained long-lasting results.

[4] David Scott Palmer, talk programme at the American Center, Kathmandu, 8 August 2003.

[5] Ibid.

CHAPTER 6

Implications of the 11 September Developments

The world and its trajectories have changed irreversibly after 11 September 2001. The horrific terrorist attacks in New York and Washington changed the content and conduct of contemporary international relations and introduced a new term, '*post*-Post Cold War period' in global politics. A growing feeling of 'we ought to contribute to enable all regions of the world to live in security and harmony, otherwise insecurity will also come to us' is widely prevalent and has contributed to an altered perspective on international terrorism, freedom struggles, poverty and *mal*-governance, coupled with state desire and capability to deal with the global menace.

So far-reaching has been the impact of the event that all regions and countries are affected directly or indirectly by the subsequent American-led 'war on terrorism'. Kajima Akira, writing for the *Gaiko Forum* published from Tokyo mentions that 'the acts of terrorism on 11 September represented the first attack on the US mainland since the founding of the nation, forcefully demonstrating to Americans the vulnerabilities of even an ultra-modern defense system' he says. 'The mammoth military power is now keenly aware of its vulnerability in not knowing when or where it could be altered.' Hence, countering terrorism became an international venture led by the sole superpower, and due to the transnational character of terrorist groups, the US felt that terrorism germinating even in a small, weak and landlocked country should be dealt with with a firm hand with necessary support from the international community. The US had long been discussing the link between unfulfilled development needs and the emergence of violence, but never had it actually stressed the link between the two with so much authority. Never was there a realization in Washington that threats to the US homeland may or may not necessarily stem from countries that possess continental ballistic missiles, nuclear or biological weapons. Small, landlocked, and poor countries could be just as dangerous.

Reaffirming its unequivocal condemnation of the terrorist acts, the UN Security Council unanimously adopted a comprehensive resolution with steps and strategies to combat international terrorism. This concerns us here in our analysis. Known as Resolution 1373, it also established a Committee of the Council to monitor the Resolution's implementation and called upon all states to report on actions they had taken. The Resolution passed on 28 September 2001, stated that:

> all States should prevent and suppress the financing of terrorism, as well as criminalize the wilful provision or collection of funds for such acts. The funds, financial assets and economic resources of those who commit or attempt to commit terrorist acts or participate in or facilitate the commission of terrorist acts and of persons and entities acting on behalf of terrorists should also be frozen without delay. [The Council also decided that] States should prohibit their nationals or persons or entities in their territories from making funds, financial assets, economic resources, financial or other related services available to persons who commit or attempt to commit, facilitate or participate in the commission of terrorist acts. States should also refrain from providing any form of support to entities or persons involved in terrorist acts; take the necessary steps to prevent the commission of terrorist acts; deny safe haven to those who finance, plan, support, commit terrorist acts and provide safe havens as well.

All these developments obviously impacted on the South Asian region, and subsequently on Nepal. American military intervention in Afghanistan to remove the Taliban from power further altered the existing regional dynamics by upsetting the local balance of power and even forcing Pakistan to harden its stand against the Islamic hardliners in its territory. Its unilateral attack to oust the Saddam Hussein regime succeeded both in capturing the former dictator and setting up an interim administration in Iraq, proving that any country placing itself at the wrong end of the world's sole superpower would have to pay a heavy price.

At the end of November 2002, the US Congress passed a Bill to create a Homeland Security Department with a staff of over 1,70,000 employees. Amidst great tension in the region and the ongoing hostility between India and Pakistan reaching a new high, the 11th SAARC Summit held in Kathmandu in January 2002 accepted UN Resolution 1373 as the basis for future actions against terrorism, and stated that all the seven member states were determined to 'redouble efforts, collectively as well as individually, to prevent and suppress terrorism'. Nepal, as the host country, proposed this declaration to be passed by the Summit.

In the aftermath of the events, and with the tough lessons learnt, there has been a more realistic and sensible approach to confronting threats without double standards. Individual countries were quick to utilize the 'favourable' global environment in order to deal with their own enemies back home. The LTTE, HAMAS, Chechen rebels, Kashmiri Mujahideen were no longer viewed as freedom fighters, but were instead bracketed in the term 'terrorists' not only by Sri Lanka, Israel, Russia, and India, but even by the US. The entire civilized world found no option other than to follow the policy adopted by the Americans. Perhaps the best aphorism came from the French daily *Le Monde* which carried a banner headline 'We are all Americans'! Although there is no internationally accepted definition of the word 'terrorism', yet there is widespread anxiety that in the rush to tackle terror, civil liberties have been, or may be, curtailed. But one thing is certain: Yasser Arafat's proclamation, 'Nobody is a terrorist who stands for a just cause' is outdated and an antithesis to today's scenario, which has shifted focus from issues like freedom movements to more pressing issues of international terrorism.

The Sher Bahadur Deuba Government at the time was prompt in seizing the opportunity of the post-9/11 developments to muster its strength both in diplomatic and military terms.

India, China, the US, Britain, Japan and many other friendly countries condemned the Maoists and expressed their unequivocal support and sympathy with Nepal's fight against the armed Maoist militants. Within a very short period, Nepal witnessed hectic political, diplomatic and security activities manifested in the visits of high-level dignitaries and other officials having political and security consultations.'[1]

Gen. Colin Powell visited Nepal in January 2002, the first visit ever of an American Secretary of State, underlining the importance the US was beginning to attach to Nepal. Apart from an audience with His Majesty the King and a meeting with the prime minister, Powell also visited the Army HQ where he was briefed on the ongoing counter-insurgency operations. Powell, who had two stints of active duty in Vietnam during the Maoist rebellion there, renewed the US government's strong support for Nepal's military action against the Maoists, reaffirming that there was no room for use of violence to force political change in a democracy. He said that the US fully acknowledged Nepal's right to protect its citizens and institutions from terrorist attacks.[2]

Two months later, a high-level military assessment team from the Hawaii-based Pacific Command visited Nepal and travelled to some Maoist-hit areas. On 30 March 2002, State Department Deputy Spokesman Philip Reeker urged the Maoists to lay down their arms immediately and stop brutal and senseless attacks against civilians and 'to engage in peaceful pursuit of their aims within the democratic framework of Nepal's Constitution'. Ten days later, India and the US held a major brainstorming session on the insurgency in Nepal and the reconstruction of Afghanistan. Discussions on Nepal were held between the visiting US Assistant Secretary of State for South Asia, Christina Rocca and, Joint Secretary (North) at the Indian Ministry of External Affairs, Meera Shankar.[3] Extensive consultations between India and the US came about after the US made it clear that the Maoist insurgency fell within the sphere of its global campaign against terrorism. After

[1] Krishna P. Khanal, 'Post-11 September Developments and Nepal: Implications for Curbing Maoist Insurgency', in *South Asia and the War on Terrorism*, ed. Dipankar Banerjee and Gert W. Kueck, New Delhi: RCSS, p. 31.

[2] Ministry of Foreign Affairs of Nepal: www.mofa.gov.np

[3] 'India, US Discuss Nepal, Afghanistan', *Hindu*, 10 April 2002, p. 5.

11 September, although Indian strategic analysts would not be too pleased with growing American involvement in Nepal, any indication that they were being uncooperative would expose, yet again, its image of being a regional bully.

As a by-product of these visits and the quiet diplomacy exercised by Nepal by sending its Foreign Secretary, Madhu Raman Acharya, to the US and the UK, the US agreed in principal to provide military hardware worth US$20 million to Nepal. American interest in Nepal shot up markedly following the 9/11 developments. At a working lunch with a few Nepalese editors during her official visit to Nepal in December 2002, Christina Rocca stated that 'America is committed to help Nepal combat the Maoist insurgency by providing security assistance'. She lashed out against the Maoists who had only recently owned responsibility for the murder of two Nepali security guards at the US embassy.[4]

Support and cooperation from India, China, and the US related particularly to the supply of military hardware, and were issues of great significance because the RNA was not equipped to deal with a highly motivated rebel group, a difficult terrain and poor intelligence. America invited more and more soldiers and senior police officers for training in counter-insurgency, while India went to the extent of saying that the 'Sky is the limit in supporting Nepal to counter the Maoist insurgency.' So much so that the Chief of the Army Staff of the RNA, while briefing the King, Crown Prince and the newly appointed ministers of the Chand Government which was constituted after the royal move of 4 October 2002, said that 'India has done a lot in assisting the RNA in hardware supply and training.'

Prime Minister Deuba visited America in May 2002 to garner support for what he termed was 'Nepal's war on terror'. In a speech at the Asia Society in New York on 10 May, he said:

> We value democracy and freedoms as our fundamental rights, cherish constitutional monarchy as the unifying symbol of the nation. And want to

[4] M.R. Josse, *Nepal: Politics of Stalemate, Confusion and Uncertainty*, Kathmandu: People's Review Publishers, 2003, p. 20.

bring about pro-people socio-economic progress. It is sad that Nepal, famous for its stupendous natural beauty and friendly people and an independent and peaceful country through the ages, has to pass through this very difficult phase.

In December 2002, an agreement between His Majesty's Government of Nepal and the Government of the United States of America regarding the surrender of persons to the International Criminal Court was signed by Foreign Secretary Madhu Raman Acharya and American Ambassador Michael E. Malinowski in Kathmandu.

After the first round of negotiations between the Chand Government and the Maoist rebels, the American government listed the Maoists as among 38 outfits under what it named as 'other terrorist groups'. Explaining this move in between negotiation parleys, Ambassador Malinowski said that 'a major portion of US foreign policy was directed towards anti-terrorism and that the Maoists have to prove by their action whether to come out of the list of terrorist groupings'.

With the UK too, the events of 9/11 drew up a more concretized relationship based on democracy, good governance, and human rights. The UK has always maintained that the insurgency—although with a terrorist tinge—also has economic, political, and cultural dimensions to it that have long been neglected by Nepal. It, moreover, stressed that a military solution to the problem was neither likely nor should be experimented with. This was perhaps the reason why it donated two helicopters specifically for the purpose of supplies and humanitarian aid, but not for combat. Parliamentary Under Secretary of State Mike O'Brien visited Nepal soon after the royal proclamation of 4 October 2002. In an interview to *The Kathmandu Post* he lambasted the Maoists and said that:

> the terrorists must get this lesson very clearly that the international community will not allow them to win. It is not possible for them to win. No matter how much they kill people, murder people, victimize people, abuse

people, infringe their human rights, the international community will not allow terrorism to overtake Nepal.[5]

Furthermore, the UK appointed Sir Jeffrey James as Special Representative to Nepal on 24 February 2003 in the context of the government–Maoist ceasefire. He visited Nepal several times and had interactive sessions with a wide spectrum of political leaders.

The post-9/11 scenario has been worrying for insurgencies all over the world, and there is tremendous pressure that all acts of violence must be dealt with strictly and with force. Religion, ethnicity, nationalism, economic deprivation—nothing has been given the privilege to justify a violent act of terrorism. Perceptibly, what is crucial is to assess the unfolding interest of the world's only superpower in Nepal, where American presence in terms of both tacit and open intervention can change the balance of power that has so far involved only India and China. Both are obviously not pleased with the growing American involvement in Nepal, be it in the name of assisting the HMG/N to tackle the Maoist insurgents, or in the guise of 'mediating' or 'facilitating' the peace process. So much so that even the roles of Switzerland, Norway, the EU, or the UN (with the fear of possible American influence) to smoothen the process of negotiations or help to create an atmosphere conducive to talks is not viewed in a positive light by Beijing and New Delhi. While directly hinting at some Western powers, China has explicitly said 'Nepal should and is capable enough to solve its own problems by itself', India has time and again put it frankly that due to the Treaty of Peace and Friendship signed in 1950, Delhi is obliged to be informed of the foreign arms and ammunition that reach Nepal from third-country sources.

The American envoy Michael E. Malinowski in an interview to Nepal Television pacified those apprehensive minds that fear big-power rivalry inside Nepalese territory by stating that 'the US is doing nothing in Nepal that would antagonize India or

[5] *The Kathmandu Post*, 12 October 2002, p. 1.

China'. Rocca went a step further and said that [the US] and Indian authorities were working together very closely as far as Nepal was concerned.

The historical aspect of the Nepal–US ties needs to be emphasized in this context. While it is true that some elements of the bilateral relations have been curtailed in the context of the above-mentioned war on terror and communist insurgency in Nepal, the US has proved to be a 'friend in need' of Nepal whether during the Panchayat or the multiparty era. Nepal established diplomatic relations with the USA even before it established official diplomatic relations with India and China. Both Peking and Delhi may have been startled, but the late King Mahendra addressed both houses of the American Congress during his state visit in 1960, a rare gesture not shown to contemporary South Asian leaders. The Americans, furthermore, assisted Nepal in its drive against possible communist subversion in the backdrop of the cultural revolution, much of which remains classified information even till today. They began military training to RNA soldiers as far back as 1983. In order to strengthen the bilateral relations and to acquaint Nepalese scholars, politicians, artists, journalists, etc., with American culture, the economy, legal system and polity, hundreds of Nepalese have visited the US under the International Visitors Program (IVP). The Peace Corps programme was started in Nepal immediately after President Kennedy announced it in the early 1960s. Thousands of these American volunteers have returned, assuming influential positions in diverse spectra of American life. Some American senators and congressmen in a strong letter to Indian Prime Minister Rajiv Gandhi urged him to lift the economic blockade of Nepal in 1988 on the pretext of the trade and transit treaties. They also stressed on strengthening democracy and democratic institutions, maintaining the freedom of the press in Nepal, and voiced considerable support for human rights causes even in the context of the counter-insurgency operations.

While receiving Their Majesties King Birendra and Queen Aishwarya at the White House lawns in 1984, President Reagan remarked, 'Nepal is a neighbor of the United States of America at the other side of the globe.' True to his visionary words, American assistance today continues very much as if it were a 'distant neighbour' that is concerned with the situation that prevails on the ground, and not merely as any other international donor.

CHAPTER 7

Appalling Saga of Human Rights Violations

Since the start of the movement, both the Maoists and the state security forces have embarked on a frenzy of killing, plunging the otherwise tranquil hills of the kingdom in a state of turmoil. Human rights violations are becoming increasingly common and a revenge approach has become the order of the day. Even the calls by international human rights watchers are being taken casually. The perpetrators are rarely punished. While the rebels proclaim that informers, feudal landlords, and enemies of the people have to be exterminated, the government, in an effort to contain situation, starts taking revenge on the insurgents—in both cases the innocent victims are the poor and oppressed people of Nepal.

Speaking in Dailekh district in 2001, the former Inspector General of Police Pradeep S. J. B. Rana admitted that maltreatment of the ordinary people by the police was the cause behind the increase of Maoist activities in the country. He acknowledged that, 'The police ill-treated the common people during its anti-Maoist operations in some hilly districts of the mid-western region two years ago.'[1]

An Amnesty International Report, *Nepal: A Spiraling Human Rights Crisis*, presents a horrific picture of a country that likes to publicize itself as *the birthplace of Lord Gautam Buddha*. 'Nepal's six-year-old people's war has generated a human rights crisis that is putting the country's future at risk,' it says, 'human rights protection has been swept aside as both the Communist Party of Nepal (Maoist) and government security forces have engaged in

[1] *The Kathmandu Post*, 19 May 2001, p. 1.

'disappearances', abductions, torture and unlawful killings. The conflict has had a grave impact on civilians.'

During Operations Romeo and Kilo Sierra Two, ignoring basic ethics and fundamental values of human dignity, the police mercilessly killed several hundred Maoists, who, should actually have been taken into custody for judicial proceedings. They could have been educated and counselled by taking various aid agencies into confidence which could have helped in this regard and then encouraged to take up other professions. Additionally, government quotas for the workforce in Malaysia, the Gulf and elsewhere could have been offered to these Maoist detainees, which would, perhaps, have encouraged others in the group to defect. The same holds true for the 'Jungle Search Operation' and 'Search and Destroy' action. 'The state justified authoritarian policies in the name of suppressing the insurgency without addressing the basic inequalities that plague the Nepali society. These police operations have applied the policy of 'encircle and kill', a policy similar to China's Chiang Kai-shek's 'extermination' of [the] communists' campaign in [the] 1930s.'[2]

There were reports of gang rapes and public tortures in the hills of the mid-west. The Maoists were quick to exploit the government blunders to their own advantage, and as a tragic consequence, scores of villagers still recall the incidents with anger. For the poor peasants and illiterate womenfolk, the police always tended to represent the state and reflected the state's overall attitude to those on the fringes.

Major methods used by the state security forces in gross violations of human rights include the following.

1. During cordon and, search and destroy operations, care is not taken to separate the innocent from the insurgents. Most of the time, this is difficult, as simple peasants in the afternoon can become deadly guerrillas at night.
2. State security personnel have not been properly oriented and briefed on human rights culture and matters. They have neither

[2] Chitra K. Tiwari, 'Maoist Insurgency in Nepal: Internal Dimensions', South Asia Analysis Group paper no. 187, p. 1.

been told that their casual approach can backfire, resulting in enormous loss of life and property, nor has there been any assessment of the general feeling of insecurity on the part of the common man as and when the security forces enter a particular area.

3. Rape and sexual harassment as well as disappearances and torture, are the main human rights abuses that occur time and again wherever the state security forces operate. Unless the perpetrators are sternly punished, they will not be discouraged.
4. With little information on the whereabouts of people taken in custody, there is always a suspicion that they have been killed. State security has never been mindful of the privileges of journalists, which frequently results in trouble and embarrassment. Journalist Krishna Sen, it is said, was murdered by state security, a news report which has been refuted by the Home Ministry but widely held to be true.
5. As the gun culture becomes rampant, soldiers have become trigger-happy, and as the state gets more and more dependent on the security forces, this appalling trend can only continue. It will only result in the erosion of people's faith in their security forces, which ultimately results in more killings and disappearances.

Amnesty International has expressed concern over reports that the army deliberately killed 19 Maoists after taking them in custody in Doramba village, Ramechhap district on 17 August 2003. A release issued by Amnesty said that 19 Maoists had been attending a meeting in a house when the security forces arrived on the scene and opened fire. One Maoist was shot dead and 18 others taken into custody. This incident received international publicity and the RNA has received flak both at home and abroad. Similarly, in Balaju, in the heart of Kathmandu, an innocent driver was killed by an RNA soldier because he rammed his vehicle into an army bus, earning all-round condemnation. With such incidents occurring regularly, the people fear that the growing militarization of the kingdom will affect the very fabric of the society. Although the RNA has constituted a human rights cell in its headquarters to oversee abuse of authority by the soldiers and educate the officers regarding the essential tenets of human rights, the situation is yet to improve. Moreover, some retired generals feel that the RNA needs to strengthen its PR skills, and dissemination of information needs to be done in a more effective and reliable manner. It is true that some International Non-Governmental Organizations (INGO) or NGOs, supposedly focusing on human rights, tend to turn anti-state or try to equate the army with the rebel groups while reporting the overall human rights situation in any country. Most of the time, however, personal relations with certain staff of those organization(s) also makes a marked difference.

As a retaliatory gesture, the Maoists too execute scores of police and army officers who are wounded, taken prisoner, or surrender. Extortion, looting, call for Nepal *bandhs*, etc., are other important coersive methods resorted to.

According to human rights watchers, the situation deteriorated since the state of emergency was declared in November 2001 and greatly improved during the peace talks between the Chand Government and the rebels. During the emergency, the state security forces arrested hundreds of people, and special counter-terrorism measures have undermined the very tenets of human rights. The Maoists, who now control a sizeable proportion of the country, have taken around 500 people hostages, tortured scores of people, and recruited child soldiers. They have targeted not only the security forces but also important infrastructure such as telecommunication network, roads, factories, and private boarding schools.

Amnesty International's report has also mentioned that 'the international community has been slow to wake up to the human rights crisis in Nepal and should offer sustained assistance to bring about a resolution. The turmoil in Nepal could exacerbate the already high regional tensions.'

A Global Report on Child Soldiers released by the Coalition to Stop the Use of Child Soldiers in 2001, says that about 30 per cent of the guerrillas involved in the underground CPN(Maoist)-led People's War are children. The report claims that Maoists are using school students and younger children for the insurgency. Six guerrillas under 18 were killed in a single encounter in 1999 in Kavrepalanchok district.[3] 'The underground Maoists have outdone the government when it comes to violating human rights during the year 2000', says a report released by Informal Sector Service Centre (INSEC)-Nepal. The rebels killed 218 people in 2002, while the number of people killed by the security forces stands at 179.

The violence unleashed by the Maoists can be summed up as under:

1. The people's courts give death sentences to informers and workers of other political parties. Abduction is common.
2. Ruthless killings of policemen and soldiers along with non-combatants have created a state of terror.
3. Looting banks and forcing 'donations' and contributions from businessmen and common people has affected the lives of all citizens.
4. Seeking to impose narrow views and beliefs on others and frequent calls for Nepal *bandhs* has resulted in blatant misuse of muscle power.
5. Destroying public property, educational institutions, telecommunication towers, drinking water pipelines and power projects that often take decades to rebuild has cost the country dearly.

Along with these, cow slaughter, forcing acquiescence of one woman to give sexual pleasures to an array of men, persuading women cadres against getting pregnant, destroying temples and stopping religious festivals, one family-one guerrilla scheme, etc., are some illustrations of the shocking acts of terror that have hurt sections of the Nepalese society, which is one of the most backward and poverty-stricken in the world.

In February 2001, underground Maoists banned all government employees and teachers working in various VDCs from travelling to the headquarters of Kalikot district. Such embargos are common, and these days, even the government security forces have

[3] 'Soon, the Children's War?', *Nepali Times*, 29 June–5 July 2001, p. 4.

announced similar embargos on food and travel in certain areas in the grip of armed conflict. The distressed people of the villages, specially from the mid-west, have found no alternative other than to seek refuge in Kathmandu and other major cities of the country. For the first time in history, the Nepalese are being displaced in their own motherland.

After touring the sites of Maoist attacks, the American ambassador Malinowski, compared the Maoists with the infamous Pol Pot regime. 'These terrorists, under the guise of Maoism or so-called People's War are fundamentally the same as terrorists elsewhere—be the members of the Shining Path, Abu Sayef, the Khmer Rouge or Al Qaida.'[4]

But the eye-for-an-eye approach taken by the government may soon leave the whole country blind. 'The fact that the daily defense ministry news bulletins refer only to dead insurgents, and rarely to the "captured wounded", is also enough to prove that few prisoners are being taken and more are being killed.'[5] The National Human Rights Commission, in its first annual report released on 1 April 2002, stated, 'The government has been reluctant towards the protection of human rights. During the process of investigation, the government has even remained uncooperative,' it alleged. Such a serious allegation from a constitutional body of the incumbent government still did not rectify the violations that were taking place.

Abusing authority in the name of curtailing the menace of terrorism and arresting 'journalist terrorists' has already invited sharp reactions both at home and abroad. But there is still a long way to go, as there is always a tendency among political leaders in the government to see terrorism and terrorists everywhere, from those inside the jungles to those that are in the party offices of rival political groups.

INSEC released the *Human Rights Yearbook 2003*, showing the grim reality of the human rights situation in Nepal for the period

[4] Speech delivered at the South Asia Peace Operations Seminar in Kathmandu, February 2002.

[5] Kanak Mani Dixit, 'Insurgents and Innocents', *Himal South Asia*, June 2002, p. 34.

1 January to 30 December 2002.[6] The appalling picture that it portrayed was that during the year, more people were killed by the State than by the rebels. Some of the most shocking revelations of the book are as follow:

1. There were more than 21,084 incidents of human rights violation: 52 per cent by the Maoists, 38 per cent by the state, and the rest by others.
2. There were 4,952 persons killed in one year-period, out of whom 3,297 were killed by the state alone. The Maoists killed 1,358 people, while others killed 297 during the same period.
3. A total of 1,35,118 violations were recorded against the International Covenant on Civil and Political Rights (ICCPR).
4. A total of 4,873 violations were against the International Covenant on Economic, Social and Cultural Rights (ICESCR).
5. Altogether 17,564 people were displaced, most of them due to Maoist threats.
6. Almost 46 under-aged persons were also detained during the period.
7. Rukum, a mid-western district, accounted for the highest number of deaths with about 500 killings, followed by Dang, Rolpa, Achham, Jumla, Salyan, Bardiya, Surkhet, Doti, and Lamjung in the top 10.

If the present human rights situation in the country keeps on deteriorating at the present pace, some analysts even fear international or UN intervention in order to safeguard the rights of Nepalese to live peaceful lives. While committed and responsible efforts on the part of the government and the Maoist rebels to respect human rights and civil liberties at all times may reduce the number of violations, international organizations such as the UN, and donor communities too, would want to assist in educating both their armies, rather than simply making headlines with appalling cases that only further terrify and intimidate the people of Nepal.

[6] www.insec.org.np/yb_2003.html

CHAPTER 8

Cat and Mouse Game of Talks

Often when military solutions do not succeed or are proved unviable, the conflicting parties agree to negotiations. The Maoists in Nepal have been demanding that the government must create a proper atmosphere for talks. On the contrary various governments, have not been consistent either in dealing with the insurgency or with the peace talks. Petty jealousy rules Nepalese politicians with the constant fear that the leader of a rival party might possibly succeed in resolving the insurgency. Hence, there is no national consensus on ways to deal with the insurgents, leaving the field open to the rebels to play one against the other. When the G.P. Koirala Government was in place, for instance, Sher Bahadur Deuba was 'a soft-liner and accommodative' to the Maoists, while Koirala was 'a defamed fascist murderer'. Within a span of six months, the tables were turned, with Koirala being termed a 'democrat' and Deuba a 'pawn of the palace'. The same holds true for the leaders and the way they view the Maoists. Koirala struggled relentlessly while he was prime minister, and the only grievance he had with the palace 'was not being able to use the army to quell the insurgency'. However, when the army was ultimately mobilized under a state of emergency, he and his stalwarts soon started calling for peaceful negotiations, and the army's return to the barracks.

Almost all the parties with a significant political base in the country have formed their own governments in the past twelve years of multiparty rule. In other words, they have also had the chance to formulate their plan of action to solve the Maoist inbroglio. Each of them have tried to deal a heavy blow on the insurgency by mobilizing the security agencies as if that was the sole solution to the problems of governance they themselves were responsible for creating. But, remarkably, the same parties showed their peaceful side by abstaining from supporting any violent suppression of the movement from government quarters as soon as they were relegated to their parliamentary opposition role.[1]

One, therefore, cannot but praise the craftines of Maoist leaders in managing political contradictions to the advantage of the revolution. The finesse with which they have played their cards with careful consideration of all the pros and cons has definitely given them at least short-term gains if not long-term political leverage. The *Prachandapath* brought out by Comrade Pushpa Kamal Dahal as a doctrine of the party tries to be as soft as possible on the demands that were high on the party's previous agenda. The document offers a way out from the present state of limbo by citing the possibility of a dialogue, and asks for a guarantee for an all-party convention, formation of an interim government representing all parties, and drafting of the People's Constitution.

However, it is a tested hypothesis that insurgencies have built-in structures to resist negotiations. In every case of militancy, decision-making is totally centralized and the top leadership leaves no room for lower level leaders, because they have their own anxieties regarding survival and erosion of power and influence in the post-settlement phase. Hence, it is not clear whether the Maoist leadership sincerely desires to end this impasse in a peaceful manner, or prolong the conflict in the pursuit of final, decisive victory and in the meantime enjoy power, influence, media hype, and authority which could be considerably reduced once the conflict is settled amicably.

Another factor that needs to be scrutinized before dissecting the various phases of failed negotiations in the context of Nepal is that of both sides having more to gain from conflict than from peace. A mutually inconsistent goal that both the state and the rebels are seeking has left little room for compromise and consensus. A good knowledge of various conflict resolution techniques, negotiation styles, illustration of other models of peace-building in multicultural societies as in the case of South Africa,

[1] Hari Uprety, 'Peace Dialogue in the Process of Conflict Resolution in Nepal', in *Conflict Resolution and Governance in Nepal*, ed. Ananda P. Srestha and Hari Uprety, Kathmandu: NEFAS, and FES, 2003, p. 234.

the Jura conflict in Switzerland, Northern Ireland, El Salvador, Guatemala, Nicaragua, and even in Mizoram, etc., could help in perhaps getting over this stalemate. A poor way of negotiations practised by Nepalese leaders is of informing the press first that 'the government is willing to talk with the rebels', and notifying the rebels later. Proper homework, coordination with colleagues, full backing and trust of political constituency are a must before initiating any such exercise. Although there are arguments on whether international mediators are needed, there is consensus on the essentiality of rigorous preparation, coordination, and use of negotiating skills from different types of conflict resolution exercises around the world.

One such seminar on 'Conflict Resolution and Peace Building in Multi-Cultural Societies' organized by the Swiss Development Corporation was held in Montezillon, Switzerland from 11–16 February 2003, in which this writer also took part. All the participants were Nepalese nationals, while the moderator and the lecturers were Swiss who had extensive experience either of living in Nepal, or of dealing with issues related to Nepal. For instance, Walter Voyame, author of the *Jura Canton's Constitution*, was in Nepal in 2000 for a private visit. Some of the SDC's personnel who were the organizers of the seminar had previously been associated with the SDC's work in Dolakha and Sindhupalchowk districts.

The seminar primarily dealt with the conflict resolution exercise in the Jura canton in Switzerland and in South Africa. It was left to the participants themselves to draw comparisons and chalk out lessons for Nepal. A country of 26 small cantons, Switzerland is a federation of states but is not a federal republic. The Swiss, it was said, are 'dearly attached with their cantons which have their own independent parliament, tribunal and government and even their own laws'. It was explained, at length, how the primarily French-speaking Jura canton separated from Berne, a German-speaking canton. Additionally, the racial divide in South Africa, the violent movement to outlaw apartheid, and the international pressure leading to a negotiated settlement were also presented before the participants. F.W. De Clerk got a referendum from the white community in order to get a clear-cut mandate to negotiate with Nelson Mandela. It proved to be a 'cunning masterstroke', after which both leaders didn't have to look for mandates. Ultimately, not only was peace restored, but the formation of the Truth Commission also helped the past to be uncovered and victims to receive compensation. The following were laid out as steps for peaceful resolution of protracted conflicts as in the case of the Jura canton and South Africa.

1. Pre-negotiations (talks about talks).
2. Building confidence.
3. Establishing conditions for negotiations.
4. Protecting the peace process.

The peaceful resolution of prolonged bloody conflicts—according to some of the speakers who had had stints as mediators—could be concluded in a phase-wise, step-by-step manner, but all the time with careful judgement to sustain the peace process and not allowing either side to leave the process. It was also emphasized that both the parties may have to lose equally during the negotiations, and both may have to leave the table equally unhappy, but negotiated settlement is necessary in the larger interest of the people. The step-by-step approach suggested is represented in Fig. 8.1.

1. Contact

   □

2. Mutual understanding and building confidence

   □

3. Joint analysis

   □

4. Optional problem solving

   □

5. Joint action

   □

6. Conflict resolution

Fig. 8.1: Steps of Conflict Resolution

Other attempts to introduce Nepali participants to conflict situations around the world and their resolution have also been taking place on a frequent basis. Perhaps, with these instances of experience and insights in mind, and empowered with necessary skills, one can hope for better results in the next arc of the learning curve. Major attempts for negotiations since the start of the insurgency in 1996 in Nepal can be established under the following clusters. What is worthwhile to analyse in each case is how the state mismanaged the initial euphoria of ceasefire and public support for peace, and how the Maoists too failed to attend to the larger interests of the people and the country in search of short-term media attention.

In the year 2000, the then deputy prime minister, Ram Chandra Poudel, met a Maoist leader of Kathmandu District Committee, and it instantly created euphoria with the hope that peace would replace widespread violence. The enthusiasm died down quickly. Sher Bahadur Deuba initiated negotiations with the rebels twice: first, when he was chairman of the High-Level Committee to Recommend on Resolving the Maoist Problem, and then as prime minister of the country in 2001.

THE FIRST ATTEMPT AT PEACEFUL RESOLUTION

During the peace talks held at the Godavari Resort, both sides vowed to resolve the impasse, but the Maoists insisted on the earlier demands of a republic, a new constitution, and an interim government. Abiding by the Maoists' demand of creating a favourable atmosphere for the initiation of peaceful consultations, the Deuba Government released 33 Maoists detained under the Public Security Act. Krishna Bahadur Mahara, Top Bahadur Rayamajhi and Agni Sapkota negotiated with ministers Chiranjivi Wagle, Mahesh Acharya, Narhari Acharya, Bijaya Kumar Gachedar and Chakra Prasad Banstola at the resort. Deuba asserted that he as prime minister could not agree to the agenda of scrapping the very Constitution under which he was the head of the government of the country.

SECOND ROUND OF TALKS

At the talks held at Thakurdwara, Bardia district, the rebels once again put forth demands for a new constitution and an interim government pending establishment of a republican state. Additionally, they put forth the demand for the abrogation of the Treaty of 1950, and pulling out of Indian troops from Kalapani, together with imposition of the work permit system, and regulation of the open border with India. Inevitably, the talks were consigned to the dustbins of Nepal's recent political history.

To go by the series of further attempt at talks, both Padma Ratna Tuladhar and Daman Nath Dhungana assisted in relentlessly trying to bring the two sides together. MP Ramesh Nath Pandey also met Prachanda and Baburam Bhattarai at an undisclosed location. Several efforts from the civil society too have produced no concrete results so far. Probably the government could embark on secret negotiations with the Maoist leadership and leak it only after at least 80 per cent of the agreement is reached.

THIRD ROUND OF TALKS

On 28 January 2003, the government and the Communist Party of Nepal(Maoist) declared a ceasefire, paving the way for peace talks and giving the nation the best opportunity till date for ultimate resolution of the problem. In a day of dramatic developments, the statement from the CPN(Maoist) expressing their willingness for a peaceful solution to the problem was soon followed by a similar statement from the government, in which it agreed to withdraw a previous order listing the Maoists as a terrorist outfit.

The statement issued by the government said it would be initiating the process to notify the international community and Interpol to withdraw the 'red corner' notices issued against scores of Maoist leaders. This, among others, was a precondition laid by the Maoist outfit before there could be any talks.

Political parties reacted differently to the truce declared by the Maoists and the government, and expressed diverse views regarding their possible participation in the peace process. Nepali

Congress (Democratic) leader and former Prime Minister Sher Bahadur Deuba ruled out any possibility of his party joining the peace process. 'The country will suffer a great loss if the government does not hold talks with the rebels cautiously,' Deuba warned.[2]

Just after the declaration of truce, Krishna Bahadur Mahara, a member of the Maoist negotiation team, said that the domestic and international situation then was conducive for peace talks. In an interview with Nepal Television on 17 March 2003, Mahara, however, admitted that international forces were not positive towards the Maoist movement since it was launched in 1996. He also said that the government too seemed more serious about the peace process this time.

By a trick of fate, a day after the interview, a high-level judicial probe commission on property (JIPC) submitted its report to King Gyanendra. The commission, led by Justice Bhairav Prasad Lamsal of the Supreme Court, compiled details of properties of over 30,500 public office bearers and government servants since 1990. Officials at the commission said that of nearly 40,000 people, they had gathered evidence against nearly 2,000 people of amassing wealth disproportionate to their incomes. Some 8,000 government employees failed to submit details of their property. Meanwhile, on the basis of the Lamsal Commission report, the Commission on Investigation of Abuse and Authority (CIAA) sent letters to President of the NC and former Prime Minister Girija Prasad Koirala, spokesman of the NC Arjun Narsingh K.C., Koirala's daughter Sujata Koirala, and co-general secretary Govinda Raj Joshi, along with several other working committee members. There was wide speculation that the CIAA would then arrest Koirala and other political heavyweights on the basis of the report.

It may be useful here to analyse the repercussions of the developments after the 4 October 2002 decision of the King to sack Prime Minister Deuba and subsequently appoint Lokendra

[2] *The Kathmandu Post*, 29 January 2003, p. 1.

Bahadur Chand in his place. While Deuba's decision to dissolve the House, postpone general elections for more than six months in consultation with all major political parties and subsequently recommend to the King to invoke Art. 127 gave ample moral, legal, and political basis to the King to take momentous decision, leaders of major parties, notably Koirala and CPN(UML) General Secretary Madhav Kumar Nepal, have since then been terming the decision as an 'unconstitutional' and regressive step. A triangular contest of one-upmanship between the palace, parties, and Maoists overshadowed the political landscape of the country, each vying to outmanoeuvre the other. The decision of the CIAA was widely viewed, therefore, as the Chand Government's ploy to grill Koirala or his daughter and wreck the already pathetic images of the political parties, specially that of the NC. They got a reprieve from public opinion as soon as the Chand Government approved a rise in petroleum prices. Student agitations, protest rallies, and tyre-burning episodes started, much to the dismay of the government. It was soon fashioned to suit the agitation against the 4 October decision of the King.

The Maoists had much to gain from this agitation as they could use it as a fulcrum to blackmail the government for the release of their prisoners, while simultaneously making public contacts, calling on various officials of diplomatic missions stationed in Kathmandu, and, as the theory of Sir Thomson goes, 'emerge hardened and solidified from the ceasefire'. During simultaneous meetings with the leaders of the nine left parties and five agitating parties, Dr Bhattarai called on the party leaders to forge a decisive struggle against the largest castle of feudalism [read the monarchy].

A 22-point code of conduct between the rebels and the government was announced on 13 March and the first round of talks held on 27 April at Shankar Hotel. It decided to form a four-member facilitator team for the talks. The team members included Damannath Dhungana, Padma Ratna Tuladhar, Shailendra Kumar Upadhyaya and Karnadhowj Adhikari. The government's apparent strategy was perhaps to engage the rebels for an indefinite period, try to build confidence through informal meetings, wear down the patience and rural support of the Maoists while, continuously building up the strength of the Army, and gradually force the Maoists to withdraw the demand of a Constituent Assembly and instead agree to a claim more acceptable to every stratum of the political milieu. However, time was not in its favour as the agitation turned violent, and although public support to the so-called 'People's Movement' of the five agitating parties was minimal, the government had to concentrate on two fronts at the same time.

On 6 May 2003, the government and Maoists agreed to hold the second round of dialogue. The date and time was confirmed after a four-hour-long meeting at the Gokarna resort attended by Maoist leaders Dr Baburam Bhattarai and Krishna Bahadur Mahara, and ministers Ramesh Nath Pandey and Narayan Singh Pun. The informal meeting was another demonstration of interest on the part of the government to iron out differences with secrecy, agree on vital issues unofficially, and then gradually try to build up confidence on both sides. Interestingly, Pandey was accompanied by Dr Bhattarai, and Pun by Mr Mahara in their respective official flag cars used by HMG ministers as they moved out of the resort, while RNA soldiers guarded the two ministers, and Maoist ADCs watched over their chiefs sitting in the same vehicles! '[The] Sincerity demonstrated by the Maoists in today's meeting has made us more hopeful that we can convert the present truce into a lasting peace', said Pandey. This was clearly the climax of the ceasefire, as the atmosphere was abuzz with rumour that a lasting solution was already sorted out, simply awaiting official agreement.

Meanwhile, Maoist prisoners Rekha Sharma, Govinda Acharya, Chandra Shrestha and others were released as a gesture to the Maoists.

The Maoists, presenting their political, social, and economic agenda in the earlier round of talks, had called for an all-party conference, an interim government, election of a Constituent Assembly, and integration of the Maoist People's Army with the RNA to form a national army under the control of the elected representatives. Their demands included sending the army back to the barracks, making known the whereabouts of the missing Maoists (including politburo member Dandapani Neupane), freeing all Maoist detainees, and forming a high-level independent body consisting of human rights activists to investigate cases of rights violations between 1996 and 2003. The rebels also demanded rehabilitation of conflict-affected people, compensation to the families of martyrs, release of prisoners of conscience, and abrogation of the Terrorist and Disruptive Activities (Punishment and Control) Act.

On the day of the talks, the Maoists suddenly appeared to be more rigid than before, and demanded that the army be restricted to a radius of 5 km from its barracks. According to them, the government agreed to this at the closed-door negotiations. Following the talks, spokesman of the Maoist negotiating, team, Krishna Bahadur Mahara, disclosed to the press that both sides had agreed upon a number of issues, including the restriction upon the army. The spokesman of the government team, Minister Pun, did not contradict this statement. He, however, chose to keep mum on the issue (hinting that the agreement had not been reached) at a television interview hosted by Bhusan Dahal of Kantipur television after the fall of his government.

The government was obviously held responsible for agreeing on something that would affect the morale of the army adversely, while making it possible for the Maoists to continue their reign of terror, even though it never officially said that such a decision was ever taken. By restricting the movement of the state army and tolerating free movement around of the rebel's militia, it obviously had to face the disapproval of the palace. Ultimately, the government spokesman, Pandey disclosed to the BBC that the 'two coordinators shall sit down and sort out the issue', which was read as denial of ever having reached such an agreement. The Maoists promptly demanded the resignation of Pandey from the negotiating team. Whether it was proper for a negotiating party to call for the resignation of a member of the other party is a different question altogether, and only history shall judge its propriety.

FOURTH ROUND OF TALKS

With the Chand Government getting marching orders, the new administration under Surya Bahadur Thapa formed a new team of negotiators—two ministers Dr Prakash Chandra Lohani and Kamal Thapa. Conceivably, with the rumour that the Thapa Government had been formed with the backdoor influence of New Delhi, and Thapa's own background of being a tough and unyielding leader, might have made the Maoists more hesitant to move about freely and linger on with the talks indefinitely. The government too wanted to move straight on to the political agenda rather than deal with other nitty-gritty issues, a move that proved disastrous to the whole peace process. At the fourth round of talks held in Nepalgunj and Hapure, the government submitted a 'road map for peace', which was rejected outright by the Maoist team. Party chairman Comrade Prachanda declared that the government's concept paper 'rendered the peace talks purposeless', and it not only failed to address the fundamental problems plaguing the country, but also 'exposed the controversy through sugar-coated pills to strengthen feudal regression that became evident after October 4'.

On 27 August, they unilaterally broke off the seven-month-old ceasefire and the subsequent peace process with the government 'for the time being', saying it had lost its relevance. In his statement, Prachanda blamed the government for the developments. 'Since the old regime has ended the utility of the current cease-fire and the possibility of [a] forward-looking way out through the peace talks, our party wants to make it clear that the cease-fire, code of conduct and the peace negotiations have lost their utility,' Prachanda concluded.

However, he reiterated his party's willingness to sit for the dialogue again 'to protect people's sovereignty and their fundamental interests', and appealed both to people within, and outside, the country to help create an atmosphere conducive to the talks. Reacting to the Maoists' decision, the people, the political parties, and the business community expressed 'shock' and urged the two sides to stick to the peace process.

TABLE 8.1: ESSENTIALS OF SUCCESSFUL NEGOTIATIONS

Soft	Hard
Participants are friends	Participants are adversaries
The goal is agreement	The goal is victory
Make offers	Make threats
Disclose your bottom line	Mislead as to your bottom line
Be soft on the people and the problem	Be hard on the problem and the people

At this juncture, it is worthwhile to observe some salient points for the persistent errors that the Nepalese negotiating processes have seen from the very useful techniques put forth by Roger Fisher and William Ury in their best-seller, *Getting to Yes*. It aptly charts out a series of positional bargaining tips which would be extremely helpful for the Nepalese negotiators to learn about negotiation techniques.

They, likewise, devise a straightforward method of negotiation that can be used under any circumstances.

1. *People:* Separate the people from the problem.
2. *Interests:* Focus on interests, not positions.
3. *Options:* Generate a variety of possibilities before deciding what to do.
4. *Criteria:* Insist that the result be based on some objective standard.

Since the Maoist movement has inflicted deep wounds on the economy, polity, socio-cultural life of the Nepalese, and even the psyche of the entire state, negotiation has to be taken as a serious business and not merely as a half-hearted exercise. As the movement stems from deep-rooted socio-economic and political grievances, the state must be willing to give concessions, experiment with available options, and go the extra mile for peace. The Maoists, on the other hand, must realize that a military victory against a twenty-first century state against the background of massive international economic and military backing is next to impossible. Sooner or later, they will have to come to an understanding to evolve a broad consensus, which may warrant their having to climb down from their previous demands. Public sympathy in their cause too can evaporate quickly in the context of killings and daylight bomb blasts. Rigid postures and inflexible attitudes, therefore, can only harm the poor Nepalese, for whom both sides are fighting a relentless struggle.

CHAPTER 9

Implications for India

HISTORICAL OVERVIEW

India has a larger-than-life presence in South Asia. Its border is connected with all the other six countries of SAARC, while none shares a border with one another. Moreover, India is a hotly-contested and debated issue in the elections of almost all the smaller states, while these countries are seldom an important election issue in India. Inside Nepal, India-bashing has always been an emblem of nationalism and the show of ones love for the motherland. Hence, even when a river criss-crosses through Indian territory and inundates a few private houses inside Nepal, it is because of 'the grand Indian design'. Or cinema halls showing Indian films are burnt and bullets shot at the protesters over a Bollywood actor's comment on the Nepalese people that he never actually made. The best explication of the Indian dilemma *vis-à-vis* its Nepal policy is that it invariably tends to be at the wrong end, whether it is active or inactive.

'Any problem that arises between two close neighbours like India and Nepal, or any other smaller South Asian country, is usually explained away in terms of India's bigness and its overbearing and big brotherly behaviour. Indo-Nepal relations are obviously unequal relations.'[1] Nepal has, in the past, and still receives, a good package of aid from India in the sectors of road and railway line construction, health, IT, water resources management, education, etc. For instance, during the official visit of Prime Minister Girija Prasad Koirala to India in August 2000, the recommendations of a High-Level Task Force were endorsed and

[1] S.D. Muni, *India and Nepal: A Changing Relationship*, New Delhi: Konark Publishers, 1996, p. 1.

directions given to implement the following new projects expeditiously: improving infrastructure and physical facilities at important border customs stations; development of infrastructure, including transportation and communications links in the adjoining districts of Nepal and India; launching a rural and community development pilot project; setting up a small/medium hydropower project in Nepal; setting up an Export Processing Zone (EPZ) near the Inland Container Depot in Birgunj; cooperation in dairy development; and cooperation in establishing a technology institute in Nepal, with information technology as one of its key components.

Besides, the attachment of the peoples of the two countries and the socio-cultural links transcend all myths, tales, and fables spanning from the time of Goddess Sita and Lord Gautam Buddha. Nearly 400 years ago, a pundit from South India was made the chief priest of Pashupatinath temple in Kathmandu, a tradition still honoured by Nepal.

> The socio-cultural factors are part of our common heritage and are playing a significant role in the mutual relations between the two countries. There is close similarity between their customs, rituals, religion and behavioral pattern that it is very difficult to make a distinction between the two.[2]

It is true that while Indo-Nepal relations have been resplendent with social, economic, and cultural interchanges that have existed from time immemorial, the political component is just one of the many attachments that we have. To quote the late I.P. Singh, former Indian ambassador to Nepal:

> Indo-Nepal relations have been going in two currents, a visible current and a very basic current, which is not so visible. The visible current sometimes may have ripples going up and down but the invisible current is guided by the links of history, geography, culture, community and family relationship.[3]

[2] M.D. Dharamdasani, 'Common Heritage and Cultural Ties', in *India and Nepal*, Embassy of India in Nepal, 2002, p. 17.

[3] Foreword, *India and Nepal*, ibid.

However, more often than not, this relationship has been troublesome as the nationalistic passions of smaller neighbours like Nepal tend to get intertwined with antagonistic feelings towards big neighbours like India—a phenomenon that is also experienced by other large regional and global powers around the world, including the US. While high-level visits, and political, economic, social, academic, and cultural attachments are the hallmarks of Indo-Nepal relations, what is also true is that bilateral relations work like traffic lights, and years of toil and effort to keep the relations above political controversies suddenly sink into oblivion. Many blame this phenomenon on the extremely intimate relationship of the two countries.

The most difficult part of the whole gamut of bilateral relations is that they get perpetually entangled in the domestic politics of Nepal, with certain sections vying to cash in on any circumstance for petty political gains. Whether it be issues of inundation and border management or water sharing for mutual benefit or simply the overall attitude towards Nepal, controversies abound.

> The question of India-Nepal relations was dragged into election campaigns by the opposition—the security treaty, trade and transit issues and the Tanakpur barrage were also utilized by the opposition, chiefly the communists, to condemn the Nepali Congress for its pro-India stance and the 'betrayal' of Nepalese interests. India was a convenient whipping boy held responsible for all Nepal's problems and for its attempts to abridge Nepalese sovereignty.[4]

Not only the communist blocs, even various factions of the NC resort to naming the Other as 'Indian agents' whenever it suits them. In the event of a statement that has been misread or wrongly quoted, decisions similar to the stopping of Indian Airlines flights to Kathmandu in the wake of the hijacking, the trade

[4] V. K. Dutt, *India's Foreign Policy in a Changing World*, New Delhi: Vikas Publications, 1999, p. 186.

treaty not being finalized till the moment of its expiry, etc., the entire political spectrum of the kingdom gets geared up for a determined sortie against 'Indian hegemonism'. The talent mastered by Nepalese politicians in the last 12 years must be stressed here—that of agreeing in private and disagreeing in public! Virtually no politician actually stands up and defends genuine Indian concerns. And at a time of crisis, everyone joins the bandwagon, true or fictitious, fashioned slightly by history and more by audience-centred rhetoric.

Thus there is no dearth of people in Nepal who feel that every ill of the country has been 'designed' or 'conspired' by their southern neighbour by recalling examples of the disadvantageous Koshi, Gandak, and Tanakpur projects, the bomb explosions carried out by Ramraja Prasad Singh, the general populace having to face tremendous difficulties following deliberate lapse of the trade and transit treaties in 1989, etc. Consequently, ever since the inception of the Maoist movement, a large section of Kathmandu's upper echelon that includes the media, academia and business persons have thought that somehow a hidden Indian hand is behind the whole affair. With India's initial support to the LTTE and the historical background of the annexation of Sikkim, there are always a few takers of this argument. This hearsay has had substantial domestic and foreign takers recently in the wake of the scandalized Lucknow meeting between CPN(UML) General Secretary Madhav Kumar Nepal and the Maoist leaders.

Due to the Maoist uprising in the rural areas and the massive awareness of self-identity and nationalism by the leaders, and from them onwards to the general population over these six years, one can assert that Indo-Nepal relations could be heading for another debacle. Therefore, India finds itself in a predicament. It is regarded as 'tacitly aiding the Maoist terrorists' by Kathmandu's intellectuals, who assert that New Delhi should be handing over the top Maoist leaders hiding in India. Furthermore, Ex-Chief of Army Staff Sachit S.J.B. Rana asserted at a programme organized by the Nepal International Centre on 22 July 2002, 'India under the Prevention of Terrorist Act (POTA) Act recently banned an organization and handed over some terrorists. However, the senior leaders are still at large there.'[5]

Quite contrary to this, the Indian police have been arresting and handing over Maoists whom they find in their territory. The latest arrest of Maoist leaders Matrika Yadav and Suresh Ale Magar in Lucknow proves that India is no longer a safe haven for the Maoists. Indian Ambassador Shyam Saran too has been saying that the Maoists are 'as much a threat to India as they are to Nepal'. All this proves that Delhi is quite aware of its difficult predicament *vis-à-vis* Nepali politics, and, instead of unnecessarily getting sucked into the conflict, India would want to assist Nepal in the energy, trade, railways and education sectors and thereby mould the excessively political psyche of the Nepalese in the economic and social areas. This way, it hopes not only to win the trust of the people and the King, but also steadily pull its small, beleaguered neighbour out from a near-financial collapse. After all, India does have an extra responsibility in this regard, as even the tripartite agreement of the monarchy, parties and the Ranas was made in Delhi in 1950 at Nehru's behest. There were also the arrests of two sisters-in-law named Savitri alias Kalpana and Manisala Rawat of Dang district along with two others from a nursing home in Bareilly, in Uttar Pradesh. 'Of late, the UP police has started to crackdown on the Maoists either taking shelter in the state or undergoing treatment after getting injured in the battle with Nepal's security forces.'[6] The Chennai [Madras] airport immigration officials recently arrested C.P. Gajurel who was going to Frankfurt on a fake British passport. It was also revealed by the Indian Embassy in Kathmandu that the Indian government had banned the Maoist front organization, Akhil Bharatiya Nepali Ekta Samaj (ABNES) under the Prevention of Terrorist Act (POTA), 2002, for indulging in anti-Indian activities and for its involvement with the Indian extreme left organizations, the MCC and People's War Group for trying to create a Compact Revolutionary Zone stretching from Nepal to Andhra Pradesh, a southern Indian state.

[5] 'Army Needs to be Expanded: Ex-Chief', *Himalayan Times*, 22 July 2002, p. 1.

[6] 'UP Police Arrests Five More Maoists', *The Kathmandu Post*, 23 July 2002, p. 1.

It raises a very important question: What kind of anti-India activities was the ABNES engaging in? That the Nepalese living in India have set up several organizations is a known fact, and that a few of them are affiliated with the Maoist leaders primarily due to the influence of Bhattarai and his wife Hisila Yami is also a given reality, but as India begins cracking down on Maoist cadres and organizations in India, sympathetic Nepalese in India and Nepal may obviously be annoyed. For that reason, while there is a growing demand for India to arrest top Maoist leaders, New Delhi loses face even among Maoist cadres in Nepal, hence finds itself in a very tricky situation. It is this quandary that is likely to be a headache for New Delhi, as Nepal is in all likelihood headed for more turbulent times.

INTERLUDES OF EMBARRASSMENTS

Stratfor, the Austin-based internationally reputed intelligence firm described by *Jane's Intelligence Review* as a 'reliable barometer on what the USA thinks', and declared by *Time* as 'among the firms making the biggest splash in this new world', while publishing a special report on Nepal on 4 January 2001, stated, 'Nepal is likely headed toward even more difficult times with the probable change of its entire political system, from multiparty democracy to communist state.' It further elaborates:

> This will give a dramatic advantage to Beijing's geopolitical position on the continent while causing major problems for India. Whether the future Nepal government becomes Maoist or communist, the government will likely lean toward Beijing and will allow for establishment of Chinese surveillance and listening posts that would position China's forces close to New Delhi and other vital Indian centers. It would also help Beijing gain geo-strategic leverage over not only India but also larger areas from Central Asia through Southeast Asia. China's presence in Nepal would also complicate positions of the US Navy in the Indian Ocean. With early warning, surveillance, intelligence and navigation systems in Nepal, Beijing would keep a vast part of Asia and military forces there under constant electronic watch.

This analysis may sound a little far-fetched to those in New Delhi who are abreast with the daily happenings in Kathmandu, but the undeniable challenge is of the internationalization of the Maoist uprising in a country that has long been characterized as 'a part of the Indian security umbrella'. A portion of the inner umbrella getting drenched with the torrential rain could possibly paralyse the entire umbrella if it takes the whole problem of the rain too lightly. Ambassador A. Peter Burleigh, who served in the US mission in Kathmandu nearly 20 years ago, mentioned candidly in a talk programme in New York in the second week of June 2002, 'During my recent visit to Nepal I met a person who had met Baburam Bhattarai at a house in New Delhi. If that person can meet him, I am sure the Government of India can do the same. For that reason, India has a major role to play in resolving the Maoist problem in Nepal.' During the same interaction, Saubhagya Shah, a Nepali student at Harvard University, explicitly asserted that India's policy contra to the Maoists is very unclear.[7] To go back to the prognostication of Stratfor, it is worth noting that an Austin-based research organization wouldn't have been interested in a tiny country in South Asia provided that it didn't, in the first place, have an interesting story to hitch to India and China, the two military and economic giants of the new millennium. At the same time, as there is always a section that perpetually blames India for all the ills in Nepal, and keeping in mind its rather infamous sobriquet of a 'regional bully' in South Asia, this issue is likely to remain an embarrassment to India.

In 2002, some prominent leaders of the left parties, including the leader of the opposition Madhav Kumar Nepal, and the then CPN(ML) General Secretary Bam Dev Gautam met Maoist leaders in Siliguri in West Bengal. Since then there has been a buzz that top Maoist leaders are indeed living in India. Prior to this meeting, C.P. Mainali of the CPN(ML) also met the top two leaders of the CPN(Maoist) in Siliguri. During the visit of Prime

[7] Akhilesh Upadhyaya, 'Indian Policy Towards Maoists Not Clear: Former US Envoy', *Kantipur*, 10 June 2002, p. 1.

Minister Deuba to the US, a statement from the Maoists avowed that they wanted to hold talks with the government. Immediately after the rejection of the offer by Deuba, a Maoist leader telephoned the BBC office in Delhi and contradicted the view of the Maoists having sent the statement in the first place. Interestingly, according to the BBC, the telephone call was made from Delhi itself.

In the first week of June 2002, former prime minister and president of the NC, G.P. Koirala, unexpectedly landed up in Delhi from a visit to China. *The Kathmandu Post* of 9 June 2002 stated in a banner news report:

> India's controversial Minister George Fernandes has emerged as a self-appointed mediator between Nepali Congress (NC) president G.P. Koirala and senior Maoist leaders who are living in India. Former Prime Minister Koirala, who is currently in New Delhi has had a series of talks with Indian Defence Minister Fernandes since he arrived in Delhi.[8]

The report was immediately refuted by Koirala and also by the Indian embassy in Kathmandu. But the damage was already done, as Fernandes is well-known for his close contact with the rebels from Myanmar and Tibet.

As this series of awkward incidents continues, Indian authorities have said time and again that Nepal could inform them of hideouts of Maoist leaders in India, which would make it easy for the GOI to take action. On the other hand, the GOI has asked nine states to raise special task forces to crack down on Maoist groups, specially those operating along the open border. The proposed police forces would also concentrate on severing all links between Indian and Nepali Maoist groups. It is said that the police chiefs of Andhra, Bihar, Chhattisgarh, Orissa, Jharkhand, Madhya Pradesh, and West Bengal agreed to the Indian Home Ministry's proposal.[9] But news reports that tend to embarrass

[8] 'Fernandes Mediates between Koirala and Maoists', *The Kathmandu Post*, 9 June 2002, p. 1.

[9] Joseph Nathan, 'Indian Special Force to Crack Down on Maoists on Border', *Himalayan Times*, 12 June 2002, p. 1.

India both in Nepal and internationally continue to crop up despite its efforts to aid Nepal in this hour of crisis.

IMPLICATIONS FOR INDO-NEPAL BORDER RELATIONS

Nepal and India, apart from sharing the same cultural and religious heritage, also share an open border, which has long been a symbol of the close affinity between the two countries. With all these developments taking place, nearly 1,800 km of porous border has been transformed into a haven for smugglers and terrorists, who use the border for their nefarious and, sometimes, even dangerous activities. For the last one decade, India has been sensing threats to its security from disruptive elements making use of the open border to create disturbance in its territory which, it says, is mainly 'the handiwork of the ISI'.

Just a week before the arrival of the world's only Hindu monarch in his country (June 2002) on a state visit, a powerful leader of India's Hindu-nationalist Bharatiya Janata Party revealed that two Muslim extremist groups, *Laskar-e-Toiba* and *Jaish-e-Mohammad*, have set up bases in Nepal. The two organizations were alleged to have carried out the attack on the Indian parliament in December last year.[10]

During the visit of Nepalese Prime Minister Sher Bahadur Deuba to India, *The Hindu* (New Delhi) disclosed that there had been a secret meeting some time earlier between the Maoist representatives and the ISI in Pokhara. If indeed this is true, there are mounting concerns for New Delhi from the escalating movement.

Additionally, a new concern was already being examined: Chief of the Information Bureau of India K.P. Singh had said on 5 September 2001 in the presence of the then Union Home Minister (later also Deputy Prime Minister) L.K. Advani, Cabinet Secretary T.R. Prasad and other top-level politicians and bureaucrats that 'relations between India and Nepal were under threat

[10] 'India's Nepal Policy Confused and Convoluted', *Spotlight*, 21–7 June 2002, p. 10.

from fresh ties forged by leftist insurgent groups in the two countries'. His observation came following Naxalite groups all over South Asia having announced the formation of a Coordination Committee of Maoist Parties and Organizations of South Asia (CCOMPOSA) in July 2001. India herself has been waging a difficult counter-insurgency operation against radical leftist groups in Bihar and Andhra Pradesh, and not much is known of their activities to the GOI itself, but this was the first formal regional partnership among Maoist parties; some have even termed the organization as the 'SAARC of the Maoists'. True to the SAARC spirit, it is understood that there is animosity between the MCC and the PWG, but at the same time:

> what has raised concern is that the most dedicated Naxalite groups in India, the PWG and the MCC have gained prominence due to their ruthlessness, firepower and popular support. Large tracts are virtually under their control where they run a parallel government. Andhra Pradesh is the main area of operation for the PWG, though it is also found in Maharashtra, Uttar Pradesh, Chhattisgarh, Madhya Pradesh, Karnataka, Tamil Nadu, Orissa, West Bengal and Kerala. The MCC operates primarily in Bihar and Jharkhand.[11]

Dr Baburam Bhattarai, who holds the position of the chief of the Foreign Relations Department of the Maoists, maintains:

> CCOMPOSA has been launched to unify and coordinate the revolutionary process in the region. As South Asia is developing into one of the most potent volcanic centers of revolution in the twenty-first century, this initiative of the CCOMPOSA has been very timely and significant. We are all strengthening and expanding CCOMPOSA which is destined to play a historic role in the South Asia region.[12]

Not only the extreme left parties of India and Nepal, but even the like-minded parties of Bangladesh, Sri Lanka, and Pakistan are members of the organization. The CCOMPOSA comprises not only the PWG, MCC, Revolutionary Communist Centre of

[11] Mallika Joseph, 'Security Threat Assessment of Naxalites in India', Article no. 541, 15 August 2001, Institute of Peace and Conflict Studies (IPCS): www.ipcs.org

[12] Interview with *Nepali Times*, 13–19 July 2001, p. 5.

India (Maoist) from India (all Indian outfits), but also the Purba Bangla Sarbahara Party and Bangladesh Samaywadi Party (ML) and Communist Party of Ceylon (Maoist) from Sri Lanka, besides the CPN(M).

Previously, the MCC and PWG were the wellsprings of motivation for the Nepalese Maoists with whom the Maoists were more than eager to establish close contacts. Both organizations possess a well-trained People's Guerrilla Army which is active in places like Dandakaranya, northern Telengana, Bihar, and Jharkhand. Now it appears that the progress of the movement in Nepal and the massive international media publicity that it has received have made the Nepalese Maoists a motivation factor for like-minded groups elsewhere, including Bihar and Andhra.

Their efforts at cooperation amongst themselves already seem to be bearing results. For example, the Lucknow edition of the *Hindustan*, quoting Indian intelligence sources, reported that 'Maoist rebels are believed to have obtained a large amount of sophisticated weapons equivalent to Rs. 55 million from India's People's War Group.'[13] The insurgency-affected areas of Nepal in Kanchanpur, Kailali, Bardia, and other districts of the Terai are close to New Delhi—closer than any insurgency-hit area in the whole of India, and therefore this raises concerns about India's vulnerability hence, this raises the Indian military sensitivities.

> As the Maoists in Nepal are now collaborating with some other separatist movements such as the Khumbuwan Liberation Front in the far eastern hills, the possibility of involvement of separatist movements in the northeast with that of Maoists will endanger Indian security, especially in the sensitive 'Chicken's Neck' area near Siliguri in India where a narrow strip of Indian territory links [the] northeast with [the] rest of India.[14]

Lately, the Maoists have heightened their campaign in the Terai by exploiting the long-standing Tharu resentment. On 9 July 2002, they struck Akalgharuwa in Shumshergunj VDC in Banke (which is a border district), killing several people in a macabre manner

[13] *Hindustan*, 27 February 2002, p. 8.

[14] Prakash A. Raj, 'Maoist Insurgency and India', *The Kathmandu Post*, 9 April 2002, p. 4.

and looting and burning several houses. More recently, there have been blasts in Birgunj, a bordering business town. The Terai, known for its fertile land, forests, and comparatively affluent people, has lately had a massive population inflow both from India and the hilly districts, coupled with reduction in agricultural production due to floods, land inundation, etc. But if the insurgency is going to spread into the Terai, as in the Bheri zone which adjoins Bahraich district of India, or even to districts like Achham which is just one district away from the Indo-Nepal border, the entire Indo-Gangetic plain can be seriously affected, as no other uprising in India is as close to New Delhi as the violence in the south-western belt of Nepal will be.

> Even if the security forces are able to drive the Maoists out of the hills of Nepal, the guerrillas will simply head off to their hideouts in India. What this also means is that Nepal's security concern would span the Indian plains, where both the problem and solution may be hiding.[15]

There has always been an influential school of thought in Kathmandu that recommends that the open border should be sealed off, or at least regulated, to check an increasing number of Indian workers from entering Nepal. With the hijacking of IC-814 and growing Indian demand 'to check ISI-sponsored terrorists sneaking through the open border', this proposal has received backing even from certain sections in Delhi. But the people across the two sides of the border attached by matrimony, kinship, and commercial interlinkages will undoubtedly face tremendous hardship if passports/ID cards are made compulsory in any type of a regulating 'arrangement' between the two countries. This will definitely modify the existing characteristics of the border relationship of the two countries. The GOI's decision to deploy the paramilitary along the open border comes in the wake of the belief among the Nepalese that the Maoists are indeed using Indian territory. Former Chief of the Indian Army Staff

[15] Pushkar Gautam, 'Borderline War: Nepal's Maoist War could Spill Over into India', *Nepali Times*, 1–7 March 2002, p. 3.

Gen. S. Padmanabhan outlined while on a visit to Kathmandu, 'As far as I am concerned the border has been traditionally an open border. And this open border is being misused by a lot of people.' He also said that this misuse should be checked by the intelligence apparatus, one-to-one connections between the police on either side, and some regulation of traffic along the main routes, so that the clandestine movement of explosives can be stopped.

The Nepalese security forces too, have been extra-vigilant on the feeder roads along the border ever since the imposition of emergency in November 2001. Therefore, while it is said that the border has been used by people for anti-Indian activities, it has recently been exploited by Maoist rebels, strengthening the conviction that this border ought to be regulated for the benefit of both countries. This could alter an important facet of our relationship which, as mentioned above, has not only existed for a long time but also endured the test of time. During the turbulent period of 1989–90, Nepalese smugglers used the open border to illegally bring in much-needed petrol, diesel, and kerosene to the embarrassment of the Kathmandu administration. When K.I. Singh staged an armed revolt against the state, Kathmandu had asked for Indian assistance to arrest him. Taking advantage of the open border, the Indian police arrested Dr Singh and handed him over to the Nepalese authorities. It is not that the open border has given Nepal only contraband and criminals: there are advantages of the flourishing trade in the border towns like Birgunj, Biratnagar, Nepalgunj, and Bhairahawa. Trade in cheap Chinese products which come from Khasa to Kathmandu and then on to the Indian heartland would be jeopardized once the border is regulated, affecting the livelihoods of thousands of Nepalese who have prospered through this lucrative business. The same holds true for other products coming in from third countries and then travelling on to India. However, strict regulation and vigilance, not a total sealing off, could be worked out between the two sides in checking disturbances, while at the same time easing the lives of the people in the border areas.

SENSITIVE CHICKEN'S NECK AREA AND THE TROUBLED NORTH-EAST

The remote states of India's north-east are the country's most violent and heavily patrolled areas after Kashmir. The strategic buffer between the Indian subcontinent and South-East Asia has been afflicted by decades of separatist insurgencies which have not only affected the economy of the region adversely, but, according to *Asia Week*, 'has also claimed nearly one life a day in the past four decades'. The ULFA and BODO militants have made use of Bhutanese territory as well, thereby threatening the kingdom's relations with India. Only lately has Bhutan cracked down on ULFA militants on their bases inside Bhutan. 'The Nepalese Maoists are also attempting to establish a network in North Bengal and Sikkim. Their imperative is to develop a nexus with the PWG which is trying to build a safe corridor from Bihar to Nepal through Burdwan and north Dinajpur districts.'[16] Professor Dhruba Kumar of Tribhuvan University in Nepal feels that:

> if the terrorists of the North-East establish some kind of link with Afghanistan and the Golden Triangle and Mekong Valley and the state of Molucca in the east and the LTTE further south, terrorism will pose a great threat. As most Afghan warlords are now fighting in Jammu and Kashmir, one cannot rule out the possibility of their expanding links with insurgents in western Nepal.[17]

Confirming this fear, it has been reported in an interview in *Spotlight* that Bamdev Chhetri had visited Jammu in September 2002 to establish contact with Kashmiri militant groups for procuring arms for the CPN(Maoist).[18]

The growing association of the insurgents of the region with the Nepalese Maoists and with ULFA, while posing a security threat to India, may also pave the way for the one hundred thousand idle Bhutanese refugees to get motivated for a decisive

[16] L. Kanchan, 'Maoist Insurgency and Indo-Nepal Border Relations', article no. 678, IPCS: www.ipcs.org

[17] Dhruba Kumar, 'Regional Initiatives Against Terrorism Required', interview to *Spotlight*, 21 September 2001, pp. 22–3.

[18] 'India Suspects Maoist links with Kashmiri Militants', *The Kathmandu Post*, 17 July 2002, p. 1.

insurrection against Thimpu. There were reports that Thimpu actually used ULFA to flush out the Lhotsampas in the early 1990s. It is sheer luck that a nexus between the refugees and the Maoists hasn't yet been established, but that could simply be a question of time, as the Maoists have already made an entry into Nepal's eastern districts of Sankhuwasabha, Khotang, and Jhapa. It is in Jhapa where most of the refugee camps are situated. This district is also close to the strategic 'Chicken's Neck' area where a tiny piece of Indian territory (Siliguri and New Jalpaiguri) separates the conflict-torn states of Assam, Tripura, Nagaland, and Manipur from the rest of India. If the rebellion spreads into this region, the entire area, which already harbours one of South Asia's worst and longest-standing insurgencies, can literally go up in flames.

Nepal's Maoists have set up an improvised helipad in the thick jungles of Bihar and are using choppers to transport weapons and cadres, according to the *Himalayan Times*, a news report that has been denied by the Defence Ministry of Nepal. The news report, quoting the intelligence wing of the Bihar police, says that the rebels had set up training camps in the jungles of East and West Champaran districts, and were regrouping with help from their Indian counterparts.

The open Indo-Nepal border may now have to be subjected to new arrangements, although no one knows for sure whether the arrangements can actually prevent the movement of unwanted elements or its use for suspicious activities.

IMPACT ON THE GORKHA CONNECTION

The Gorkha connection between the two neighbours goes back 200 years when Maharaja Ranjit Singh recruited Nepalese soldiers for the Sikh army. After Independence, India retained six regiments and transferred four to the British Army. They have served with honour in Kargil and Siachen and the troubled North-East, and from Congo to Sri Lanka, with awards such as the Param Vir Chakras, Ashoka Chakras, being bestowed on them not to mention the global fame for their bravery, daring, and relentless spirit. With their war cry '*Jai Mahakali! Ayo Gorkhali!*' (Victory to Mahakali [the Goddess]! The Gorkhas are Coming!), even their favourite weapon, the *khukri*, has become world famous, with many stories and myths surrounding it.

> Gorkha units of the Indian Army have traditionally been family affairs. A battalion would generally have large numbers of troops from one or two particular villages. Units would also have large numbers of close relatives thus increasing their cohesiveness. There are many serving soldiers today who can trace their lineage through several generations of service (and several battles) in the same unit. Thus, Gorkhas see service in the Indian Army more of a continuation of tradition rather than as merely job opportunities.[19]

As of now, there are 60,000 Nepalese serving in the Indian Army, along with 1,15,000 pensioners dependent on the military pension branch at the Indian Embassy in Kathmandu. There are 20,000 additional pensioners of Nepalese origin drawing pensions from various government treasuries of the GOI. The annual remittances, plus the pensionary and welfare grants, total well over 1,000 crores in Indian currency, which has undoubtedly been a great help to the Nepalese economy. If one examines the overall Indian assistance to the Nepalese economy holistically both directly and circuitously, it is certainly a huge figure.

A long-drawn out conflict in Nepal can have serious implications for this connection which has long been a unique characteristic of Indo-Nepal relations. Since these soldiers and the Maoist rebels-in-arms are more or less from the same clans, the possibility of sisters, brothers, nephews, or even the wives of Gorkha soldiers getting involved in the Maoist rebellion cannot be ruled out. This deserves special merit, as a British Army or Indian Army soldier is comparatively richer, looked up to with respect in the villages, and everybody knows the families which have their sons in the Lahur very well. In fact, the soldiers of the RNA, the British Gurkha, the Indian Gorkha, and the lower-level force of the Nepal Police and the armed police are kinsfolk. It is said that 600 new recruitments were made in 2003, but

[19] 'The Gorkha Connection', *India and Nepal*, op. cit., n. 2 above, p. 62.

recruitment camps which were set up in Taplejung, Dhankuta, Gaighat, Okhaldhunga, Solukhumbu, and Diktel have been shifted to the Dharan main recruitment camp due to the Maoist problem. During his visit to Nepal, Gen. Padmanabhan told a gathering of ex-Indian Gorkha soldiers in Pokhara that they should always be loyal to Nepal and should not help the Maoist insurgents in any way. It has been speculated that some veterans of the British and the Indian Army, with their skills and experience in jungle warfare, are training the Maoist guerrillas: the pension privileges of two such Indian army veterans were stopped for allegedly assisting the rebels and the news was reported in the press. Maj. Gen. Ashok K. Mehta (retd), speaking at an interaction programme at the United Service Institution of India on 16 September 2002, said that several such cases have been reported. A retired sepoy of the 2/11 Gorkha Rifles, Jagat Bahadur Sunwar, and Lance Naik Ratna Bahadur Gurung were stripped of all their privileges in April 2002.

Chief of Pension Bureau Maj. Amit Kumar Chatterji was reported as saying that any Indian Army retirees or their family members assisting the rebels would be stripped of their privileges.[20] Gen. Padmanabhan pledged a support package of weapons such as small arms, armaments of various types like mortars, ammunition for small arms and mortars, vehicles, helicopters, etc., to the RNA in order to combat the insurgents. Therefore, it appears that the implications of a sustained battle in Nepal have been studied and carefully mulled over by the Indian Army, specially as regards the Gorkha connection between the two countries. The assistance only centres around arms and ammunition and providing training to Nepalese soldiers, and not the help of Indian military personnel in resolving the Maoist issue, as it will put the loyalty of a Gorkha soldier to test. Maj. Gen. Mehta, who was trekking in mid-western Nepal when the insurgency began in 1996, recommended at the same seminar at the USI in Delhi that the GOI should be willing to provide 10,000–20,000 Indian Gorkha soldiers to resolve the insurgency. This would not only be a big

[20] Harsh Subba, *Kantipur*, 31 May 2002, p. 1.

gamble, but also very risky, as the whole insurgency could then metamorphose into an anti-Indian nationalistic battle.

IMPULSE TO THE NEPALESE DIASPORA

Nepal's borders extended to Kumaon and Garhwal prior to the Treaty of Sugauli concluded with British India in 1816 following the defeat of Nepalese forces to the British Army. There has been a persistent academic debate that that territory should have been handed over to Nepal after India's Independence in 1947, as it was lost not to India, but to the British Empire.

The actual number of Nepalese (either ethnic or recently migrated) in India is unknown. Some have put the figure at roughly 8 million. They spread from Uttaranchal, UP, and West Bengal to Sikkim, Assam, and Meghalaya. Until recently, they were the majority population in southern Bhutan until the royal government started to push them out, despite the fact that some of them claimed to be living in Bhutan for nearly two hundred years. In Sikkim, the Nepalese appeared much after the Lepchas and Bhutias, but they migrated in large numbers and soon became the dominant community. The Nepalese now constitute more than 80 per cent of the total population in Sikkim, and the Nepali language is spoken and understood all over the state.

A median population census of as far back as 1871–2 revealed that other than the natives of India and 'British Burmah', Nepalese constituted a sizeable 87 in a total of 131 in the single district of Darrang alone in the state of Assam.[21] In Darjeeling, Kurseong, and Shillong, the Nepalese diaspora forms the majority. Affection of the population towards Nepal and the Nepalese is immense. Some of them trace their lineage to legendary battle heroes and can locate their parental home village in Nepal. The birth anniversary of poet Bhanubhakta Acharya is celebrated more passionately in Darjeeling than in Kathmandu. The Gorkha National Liberation Front (GNLF) had led an agitation demanding a sepa-

[21] W.W. Hunter, *A Statistical Account of Assam*, vol. I, Guwahati: Spectrum Publications, 1998, p. 55.

rate Gorkha state for eight years in the 1980s before it finally settled for a Hill Council arrangement and retained power in the area. The violent agitation, which grew out of the insecurity and underdevelopment of the people of the region coupled with the aspiration for ethnic recognition put forth the following demands:

1. A government notification granting true citizenship with franchise rights to all those Nepali-speaking people who migrated to India before 1950.
2. Creation of a separate state of Gorkhaland consisting of Darjeeling and adjacent areas out of West Bengal, but within the framework of the Indian Constitution.
3. Inclusion of Nepali/Gorkhali in the Eighth Schedule of the Indian Constitution.
4. Abrogation of Clause 7 of the Indo-Nepal Treaty of Friendship of 1950.
5. Establishment of a new Gorkha regiment for Indian Gorkhas only.[22]

Although the agitation has subsided somewhat the demand for a separate Gorkha state, to be created by the separation of Darjeeling from the state of West Bengal, has never been totally shelved. Moreover, even the concept of a Greater Nepal, though unrealistic, has always remained a sentimental issue mainly in Nepalese-dominated areas in India. Subhash Ghising, the supremo of the GNLF, had initially used this slogan to unite the Nepalese. Ghising had (likewise) harped upon an impractical concept of Bhutan forming part of a Greater Nepal Organization.[23] Bhutan, unlike the state of Sikkim, and of Darjeeling, has no common border with Nepal, and is completely separated from Nepal by a stretch of Indian territory. Later, the Thimpu government utilized the issue to influence the Indian government to flush out the Nepalese, saying that the pro-democracy movement in Bhutan was part of the Greater Nepal gameplan.

[22] S.R. Timsina, *Nepali Community in India*, New Delhi: Manas Publishers, 1992, pp. 49–50.

[23] Rakesh Chhetri, 'Bhutan and the Greater Nepal Organisation', *Independent*, 7 August 1991, p. 4.

During the 1960s, the concept of forming a confederation of the Himalayan states of Bhutan, Nepal, and Sikkim was mooted in academic circles. It fizzled out over the years, as it was likely to irk India.

But as the GOI tightens its grip over the Nepalese Maoists and tries to weaken their networks, it must not be overlooked that Maoist leaders have developed a sort of close bond with certain groups of Nepalese living in Bhutan, Assam, Sikkim, Uttaranchal, Uttar Pradesh, and West Bengal. It is said that West Bengal Chief Minister Buddhadev Bhattacharya's anger and the subsequent hard-line attitude against the Maoists apparently emanates from reports that the Nepalese rebels have allegedly been instigating the Nepalese in Darjeeling and surrounding areas to assert their right to self-determination pertaining to Nepalese-dominated areas like Darjeeling and Sikkim.

The then Prime Minister Deuba visited Kolkata as part of his official visit to India and interacted with the chief minister, something that his predecessors have never done. In the meantime, probably as an outcome of the visit, the West Bengal government also arrested CPI(ML) Darjeeling district General Secretary Abhijit Mazumdar, son of the late well-known Naxalite leader Charu Mazumdar, on suspicion that he was the key contact point of Nepalese Maoist leaders.

If the GOI comes to the aid of Nepal government whole-heartedly to wipe out the Maoists, there is the distinct possibility that the Maoists will use the slogan of 'nationalism' to unite the Nepalese against Indian 'hegemony'. Although Nepali has recently been recognized as one of its national languages by India, there is growing animosity between the other ethnic groups and the Nepalese population, as the Nepalese take away their jobs. A few cases of clashes have been reported from Guwahati [earlier Gauhati].

The slow but burgeoning animosity between the Nepalese and the other ethnic races in these areas could well be exploited for a larger and more volatile conflict transcending national boundaries, on racial, ethnic, and religious lines, and involving the entire subregion. This argument is accentuated by the fact that Nepalese living in India for several generations have still maintained their contacts in Nepal; they are, in spite of everything, discontented with their status and employment in Indian cities, making them an unappreciative and ungrateful diaspora that neither returns to their own country, nor integrates happily with the adopted country.

To sum up, a long-drawn-out conflict in Nepal can have the following grave consequences for India.

1. The Maoist-hit areas in the mid-west of Nepal are close in distance to New Delhi than any other existing insurgency in India. Already, with long-standing conflicts on ethnic, religious, and sectarian lines, India would not want is a critical situation to develop right next to the seat of its power. Even in a post-monarchy scenario, the chances of Nepal settling down to stability look slim. A sustained conflict in this area may gravely expose the entire Indo-Gangetic plain.
2. Unfortunately, India has placed itself in a rather difficult predicament in Nepal. To the Maoist leaders, India is going all out to help the Government of Nepal, while to the elite of Kathmandu, India is not doing enough to help bring back normalcy. Moreover, because the Maoists abstained from the entire Kalapani debate and have greatly mellowed their previous anti-Indian stand, there is a suspicion now that Delhi must be having a rapport with them. On the contrary, with the incessant supply of military hardware including helicopters and training to the RNA soldiers, along with the arrest of leaders like Matrika Yadav, Suresh Ale Magar, Bam Dev Chhetri and C.P. Gajurel, the Maoists definitely feel that the GOI is working against them in a consistant way. It is this dilemma that is the real challenge. But this is not the first time that India is positioned in a situation of 'do and be damned, don't and be damned'. Since 1950, almost every major change inside Nepal has been the result of deterioration in Indo-Nepal relations, but, remarkably, every scenario that emerges in Kathmandu has had difficulty in accommodating Delhi's concerns and interests.
3. The implications for Indo-Nepal border relations are evident.

India has already stationed paramilitary forces along the 1,800 km of the porous border. With complaints that the Maoists are misusing the border for their activities, including clandestine movement of explosives, plus an increasing number of reports of terrorists crossing over to India from Nepal, this unique characteristic of traditional Indo-Nepal relations is already the prime target. Now even the elite and academics of both the countries have begun to support closure of the open border.

4. The impact on the Gorkha connection between the two countries is another area where the conflict could have a direct bearing. Gorkha units of the Indian army have traditionally recruited soldiers from Nepal. Nepalese serving in the Indian army are doing so in some sensitive areas too. As the Maoist rebels and the soldiers in the Gorkha regiments are from the same clans, the possibility of family members getting involved in the rebellion cannot be ruled out. The Indian army recruitment camps set up at six different places had to be shifted in 2003. Though it has been going on for many years, it is now regarded as a disgrace for all Nepalese to have their 'daughters sold off as prostitutes in Indian brothels and sons getting recruited as soldiers in the Indian army'. The very fact that the two are equated shows that times are changing, and so are attitudes to old values, culture, and occupations.
5. The PWG and the MCC were once the sources of inspiration for the Maoists. Now it is the other way around. These like-minded groups of South Asia have formed CCOMPOSA. Cross-border relations of these groups, plus clandestine flow of weapons and ammunition, could be a major headache in the foreseeable future.
6. The concept of a 'Greater Nepal', although unrealistic, has always been a touchy issue. A long-drawn-out battle in Nepal could well have spillovers in the area, with a diaspora of nearly 8 million Nepalese.
7. A nexus between the Bhutanese refugees and the Maoists has not yet been established. But they are one hundred thousand in number, are idle, and are situated in the seven camps in eastern Nepal's politically volatile Jhapa district. This border

district is near the sensitive Chicken's Neck area where a small piece of Indian territory separates the two countries and harbours one of the region's longest-standing conflicts. A handshake between the Maoists and the Bhutanese refugees will clearly mean the entire area going up in flames. Recently, the Bhutan Communist Party (Maoists) has been formed in Bhutan.

8. A steady growth of 'conflict entrepreneurs' on both sides (Maoists and the government) will create a situation in which there will be vested interest groups which will want to sustain the conflict rather than resolve it. It will then be an unwinnable war.
9. A chaotic, messy, and politically confused Nepal can never be in the interest of India. Rather, a prosperous, stable, and friendly Nepal can be an asset for a growing power like India. The turmoil can be used to advantage by those elements that are inimical to India and want to use the situation for anti-Indian activities. Unfortunately, all the power centres of Nepal feel that Delhi plays parallel games and tries to keep some of its eggs in all baskets so as to benefit from either of the scenarios that emerge. It is this distrust and inner suspicion that will impact long-term strategic preparations.
10. Increased interest of Western powers including the US and the UK in increasing the efficiency of the army, providing the soldiers with training, and supplying sophisticated armoury can elevate the standard of the conflict and make Nepal a hotbed of international power rivalry. Already, the need of 'mediation' or 'facilitation' between the government and the Maoists to end the humanitarian cataclysm is being mooted either through the auspices of the UN by Secretary General Kofi Annan, opening a new vista of tremendous challenge to Delhi's long-term strategic leverage in Nepal.
11. The idea of a Constituent Assembly was first mooted by Delhi just before the fall of the Rana regime (see the section 'History of Nepal's Communist Movement'). However, after three generations, one is not certain whether this will somehow be to the strategic advantage of India. And if a Maoist

government is to assume office, what approach the Maoists will take with Beijing or Delhi is equally unclear.

12. Thousands of Nepalese are now fleeing to India for shelter from the explosive atmosphere in the villages. This massive inflow of refugees into the Indian heartland will create economic, political, environmental, and social challenges for India.

FIELD VISITS

During this author's visit to Raxaul as part of the field trip for this study, the Bihar police estimated that some 300 insurgents (both Nepalese Maoists and their Indian comrades) were currently undergoing training in the camps in Balmiki Nagar, Bagha, Barnnagar, Narkatiaganj, Sikta, Raxual, Adapur, and other places under two districts of the state. The MCC has considerable influence in 10 blocks of these two districts. Unfortunately, Bihar too has been waging a relentless battle against numerous outfits, most of them enjoying political backing. Dacoits and criminals get elected to the State Assembly, while a highly politicized and corrupt police force is both ill-equipped and ill-informed to carry out a massive operation. In addition to this, so large is the state, so stretched are its security personnel, and so immense are its problems that there is a feeling that even if the centre truly desires to assist Nepal in its crusade against the insurgents hiding in India, it would not be an easy task to hunt them down. The notorious dacoit Veerappan, hiding in the jungles of Karnataka and Tamil Nadu, remained untouched for years despite the numerous searches conducted by the paramilitary forces over the years [since killed by the police Special Task Force on 18 October 2004]. If a single dacoit could not be traced and continued to abduct eminent personalities and hold them to ransom, one can understand that India is indeed very large, and anyone can remain there without the knowledge of either the intelligence or security personnel.

Local dwellers, specially the traders and shopkeepers of Raxaul, a tiny border city of Bihar which has gained greatly from Nepalese consumers coming in for shopping, seemed ignorant of either the Nepalese Maoists or the MCC. According to Suresh Yadav, a shopkeeper of a sari shop in Raxaul, 'There are more deadly people in the state than the Nepalese Maoists and the MCC combined.' However, even middle-level police officers were aware of the movement in Nepal and the fact that Maoist cadres travel back and forth.

This author's Gorakhpur visit was far more fruitful as it is historically known to be a sanctuary for any type of armed revolutionary activities. The city is fairly large and has four quarters, Gorakhpur, Deoria, Maharajgunj and Kushinagar. Bhatahat, Khorabar, Pipraich, Pali, Khajni, and Bhelghat are so densely populated that there are 880 persons per sq. km. of tiny lanes and heavy traffic. The city also boasts of 120 allopathic, ayurvedic, and homeopathic hospitals. Thousands of Nepalese work in Gorakhpur city alone, and the sight of Nepalese youngsters working as waiters, rickshaw pullers, and in other cheap labour jobs is common. Some of them say explicitly that they sympathize with the demands for just and equitable economic growth in their motherland championed by the Maoists. One such, Ram Bahadur Ale of Achham, says that he donates at least 400 Indian rupees every month for the cause of the movement, basically because 'it is an uprising of the poor against feudal oppression that has been existent from centuries'.

Gorakhpur has more than 200 nationalized *gramin* (village) and *sahkari* (cooperative) banks, and it is a known fact that Nepalese can easily open accounts in the banks in Indian towns. With 20 railway stations, Gorakhpur is also one of the busiest hubs in north India. One can reach New Delhi within 12 hours, a service that is useful to all types of people from pilgrims and students to smugglers and revolutionaries.

The security of the city, one must admit, is in a shambles. Although there are more than half a dozen checkpoints from Sunauli to Gorakhpur, almost no security officer checks the belongings of the travellers. If the person looks well-heeled, then he/she is in trouble. The luggage, bags, and belongings will be thoroughly inspected unless a bribe is given. Some junior police personnel confide that they too have to hand over money to their seniors.

With the border security apparatus in this state, one wonders how India can taunt Nepal for allowing anti-Indian miscreants to sneak in through its territory.

In Delhi, the situation is little different. Although this author interacted with a number of Nepalese in the city, virtually no one working as a manual labourer was willing to expound on the sensitive issue of the uprising back home. Chitra Bahadur Magar, working in a canteen in the Jawaharlal Nehru University (JNU) hostel, felt that since India had banned the Nepali Ekata Samaj, it would be difficult even to meet Nepali friends at gatherings in major Indian towns. Provoking Nepalese workers has been a favourite pastime for some in India, be it with pamphlets and posters or graffiti and slogans about various political developments taking place in Nepal. On the way to Haridwar, one can see at least a dozen slogans painted on the main-street stockades supporting the Maoist movement in Nepal. So one can clearly assess that the movement in Nepal has a considerable strength among the Nepalese diaspora across the Indian hinterland. Due to a diverse array of issues, from unemployment to low wages, and from coercion to the neglect of the issues facing them, the movement has built up an image—that of a liberator from a purely feudal, Hindu oppressor of the minority, into a more progressive, fully democratic Nepal, where opportunities have been made equal for everyone. Alongside, there is also a range of Indian academics (to wit, Prof. S.D. Muni of the JNU) who have argued that supporting the Maoists may not necessarily be contravening India's national interests. In his recently published book, Muni has argued against what he says is a faulty policy of the GOI in supporting the two pillars of constitutional monarchy and multiparty democracy at a time when the two are at loggerheads with one another.

One can clearly see that the plight of Nepalese, not only in Nepalese villages, but also in Indian towns, is quite similar, except that they are employed in low-wage jobs in the latter. However, the stark poverty, their physically taxing and extremely difficult occupations of rickshaw pullers, night security guards, factory workers, pose a similar quest for emancipation and freedom.

IMPLICATIONS FOR OVERALL POLITICAL RELATIONS

On 13 December 1998, a rally was held under the auspices of the 'Solidarity to Support the People's War in Nepal' in New Delhi. It has been mentioned above that numerous sympathizers of the Maoist movement of Nepal are based in various parts of India, including the many Nepalese who are employed in restaurants, offices, and other places. This rally was the first of its kind, as various revolutionary parties in India came together to express solidarity with the armed struggle in Nepal and condemn what they called 'repression let loose by Nepal on the movement'. Several politicians of Indian leftist political parties also addressed the gathering. As an eye-opener, the HMG/N started posting two counsellors from the Nepal Police and the Intelligence Bureau at the Royal Nepalese Embassy in Delhi subsequent to the rally, and as a newly-found outlet to lambast sinister Indian designs against smaller neighbours, Kathmandu's elite quote this rally to cite the tacit Indian support to the rebellion.

On the contrary, the Maoists have managed to exploit nationalist feelings, which are fairly strong all over Nepal. In a pamphlet titled *Two Momentous Years of Revolutionary Transformation*, Comrade Prachanda brands the Nepalese authorities 'this government of Indian stooges', and Dr Bhattarai, in his *Politico-economic Rationale of People's War in Nepal*, calls his country 'India-locked', and goes on to declare that 'the biggest direct manifestation of world imperialist oppression and exploitation in Nepal is Indian expansionist exploitation and oppression'. Taking a U-turn from this, the party has now greatly mellowed its anti-India rhetoric, perhaps fearing the arrest of its leaders and hindrance to its activities.

Naturally, the foremost casualty of the overall political implications for Indo-Nepal relations could be the Treaty of Peace and Friendship signed on behalf of India by Chandreshwar Prasad Narain Singh and the last Rana Prime Minister, Mohan Shumsher Rana, on behalf of Nepal on 31 July 1950. Article 5 of the Treaty states: 'The government of Nepal shall be free to import, from or through the territory of India, arms, ammunition or warlike material and equipment necessary for the security of Nepal. The procedure for giving effect to this arrangement shall be worked out by the two governments acting in consultation.'

At the same time, the Letter of Exchange which was supposed to regulate certain matters of details of the Treaty, says: 'Any arms, ammunition or warlike material and equipment necessary for the security of Nepal that the Government of Nepal may import through the territory of India shall be so imported with the assistance and agreement of the GOI. The GOI will take steps for the smooth and expeditious transport of such arms and ammunition through India.'

Nepal even submitted a draft of a new treaty when Mr Kamal Thapa was the foreign minister, but things are at a standstill ever since. Some Indian academics still maintain that Nepal should either agree to abrogate the treaty, or accept it in toto. Whatever the case, in the light of all the major political parties vowing to replace this treaty, it is certain that the issue will remain one of the touchiest subjects between the two neighbours. Furthermore, as Nepal imports arms, helicopters, and other 'warlike' devices from third countries, one does not know how it will affect the provision of 'importing with the assistance and agreement of the Government of India' enshrined in the Letter of Exchange.

India has positioned herself in an extremely difficult position *vis-à-vis* Nepal. While for the Maoists and their sympathizers living in Nepal and abroad, India has been going all out to help the 'oppressive reactionary Nepalese government' to curb the uprising of the proletariat, on the other hand, for a sizeable section of Kathmandu's elite and foreigners, India is tacitly supporting the Maoist insurgency, as it did with the LTTE liberation struggle in Sri Lanka.

'Today [therefore] in Nepal there is no constituency for India, which once used to be very strong comprising especially of academicians who were educated in India and military personnel, who had close relations with [the] Indian Army.'[24] A breakaway from the current policy of supporting the twin pillars of consti-

[24] Mahendra P. Lama, 'The Future of India–Nepal Relations: Problems and Prospects', IPCS seminar, 15 September 2000.

tutional monarchy and multiparty democracy, and tacitly aiding the Maoist rebels to come to power has its risks, as then the entire international community, including the US, China, and Pakistan, will use this as a perfect example of Indian hegemony. It will, furthermore, put Delhi in the position of being a supporter of cross-border terrorism. On the other hand, unrelenting support to the state security without the Nepalese actually being convinced of Indian help brings to it the dilemma of being the loser on both counts. India's Ambassador to Nepal Saran understood this dilemma appropriately, when he said, at a function organized by the Young Journalist Forum in Kathmandu on 20 December 2003, that a lack of confidence exists between the two countries, and whatsoever India does is looked at with a negative connotation in Nepal.

Therefore, the present dilemma presents multiple quandaries for India, just as it does for Nepal. Only with profound acumen, correct judgement, perception, knowledge, and sagacity can an atmosphere of trust and confidence be built up, mutually beneficial cooperative endeavours take off, and a stability that is advantageous to both be guaranteed.

CHAPTER 10

Implications for China

During a visit to the US in January 2002, in a conversation with a Hispanic bartender in New York (who was also a student of political science) I was told that he had heard of some type of bloody conflict going on in Nepal, and asked what it actually was. On being told that it was a 'Maoist insurgency', his eyes flashed and he said, 'Oh! Then the Chinese must be behind it!' The biggest embarrassment for China is the fact that the rebellion in Nepal takes the name of their great leader Mao Tse-tung. They have to constantly take pains to assure naive enquirers that their country has long abandoned the policies of Mao, and that they have absolutely nothing to gain from a communist insurgency in Nepal.

The decade of the Cultural Revolution (1966–76) having held back China's economic and social progress, the post-Mao period saw the launching of a drive for modernization.'Within the changed global situation, China has [furthermore] remained faithful to its long-term goals of economic liberalization and growth, and to achieve them, it laid even greater stress on the reduction of tensions in its vicinity, and on the settlement of all political disputes through peaceful means.'[1]

It was the Deng era that, in fact, managed to give a great leap forward to the ailing Chinese economy, in which it is still making headway. Viewed from any angle, therefore, China does not profit from encouraging, financing, or assisting in any way, major trouble in its vicinity.

What is also a cause of worry for the Chinese is that despite efforts of over 50 years, Tibet still remains their soft underbelly,

[1] Maqbool Ahmad Bhatty, *Great Powers and South Asia: Post-Cold War Trends*, vol. V, Islamabad: Institute of Regional Studies, South Asian Studies, 1996, p. 32.

and a sustained conflict in Nepal, which adjoins the most poverty-stricken area of its Tibet Autonomous Region (TAR), can well be used by anti-Chinese activists. In the past 60 years, relations between China and the US and other Western countries and with India have fluctuated greatly. Such divisive issues as human rights and democracy, the future of Tibet and Taiwan, trade imbalances and illegal immigration, have fuelled intense debate over how the US and the West should deal with the most populous nation in the world—also known to be a rising economic and military power of the twenty-first century. The US has, in the past, designated Tibet as an 'occupied sovereign territory'. The Bush Administration is not particularly interested in forging special relations with China, compared to the policies of the Clinton Administration. The controversy dealing with the proposed visit of the Dalai Lama to the US must be looked at in this perspective.

Although sceptics of his analysis exist, Samuel P. Huntington, in his celebrated book *The Clash of Civilizations and the Remaking of the World Order*, has forecast that:

> The United States, Europe, Russia and India have become engaged in a truly global struggle against China, Japan and the most of Islam.... The alternative is to approach China from the west. The fighting between Russia and China leads NATO to welcome Russia in countering Chinese incursions into Siberia, maintaining Russian control over the Muslim oil and gas countries of Central Asia, promoting insurrections against Chinese rule by Tibetans, Uighurs, and Mongolians, and gradually mobilizing and deploying Western and Russian forces eastward into Siberia for the final assault across the Great Wall to Beijing, Manchuria and the Han heartland.[2]

Likewise, Eric S. Margolis, in his book *War at the Top of the World* says:

> Two nuclear-armed superpowers, China and India are locked in a growing strategic rivalry for regional mastery whose outcome will shake not only Asia, but the rest of the world. Three potentially explosive flash points between India and China are clearly evident: strategic Tibet, at the mid-point of their long, disputed Himalayan border; isolated, remote Burma

[2] Samuel P. Huntington, *The Clash of Civilizations and the Remaking of the World Order*, New York: First Touchestone Edition, 1997, p. 315.

and the waters of the eastern Indian Ocean. Of these three, Tibet is the most immediate and volatile flash point, and the very epicenter of the looming clash between the colliding ambitions of Asia's two giants. When this collision will occur remains uncertain, though a reasonable estimate is sometime within the coming ten to fifteen years.[3]

That China is progressing at an average annual growth rate of 7 per cent is a known fact, as also that its military and technological prowess are also catching up with the existing major powers of the world. A growing China with a prosperous diaspora spread all over the world will obviously threaten American hegemony in international politics. Tibet remains a potential flashpoint, basically because of the publicity that the issue of its liberation has been successful in garnering, and also due to the growing success of second generation Tibetans in virtually every field. Although Han Chinese now dominate the native Tibetans, it is estimated that more ethnic Tibetans may be living outside Tibet than within its borders. A brief account of the Tibet question and especially the Khampa movement via Nepalese territory will substantiate our analysis: 'Tibet used to be comprised of the three provinces of Amdo (now split by China into the provinces of Qinghai, Gansu & Sichuan), Kham (largely incorporated into the Chinese provinces of Sichuan, Yunnan and Qinghai), and U-Tsang (which, together with western Kham, is today referred to by China as the Tibet Autonomous Region).'[4]

After the 'peaceful liberation of Tibet', the Dalai Lama, his mother, sister, brother, three ministers, and around 80 other Tibetans crossed safely into India at Tezpur, Assam, to be greeted by Indian officials and a press corps of nearly 200 correspondents on 18 April 1959. Since then, the Dalai Lama has been living in Dharamsala in India, and the Free Tibet Movement has been an ongoing movement, with even well-known Hollywood stars as its adherents eager to promote its cause. Over the years, the Dalai Lama has not only established himself as an intellectual, a good

[3] Eric S. Margolis, *War at the Top of the World*, New Delhi: Roli Books, 1999, p. 181.

[4] www.tibet.com/glance.html

orator, and an ardent practitioner of the Buddhist faith, there has also been a sudden rise in the number of his disciples. Several of his books have been best-sellers, and as meditation becomes fashionable amongst the youth of today, it is the simple techniques of the art of meditation made famous by the Lama that they flock to.

Khampas (meaning the people of the Kham area of Tibet), with the reported support of the CIA, had made an unsuccessful attempt at an armed struggle against Chinese rule of Tibet in the early 1970s. To the horror of the Nepalese intelligence apparatus, two airfields in Syuchatar and Rasua inside Nepalese territory were used by the CIA to supply arms, communications equipment, and logistics to the 'Four Rivers and Six Mountain Protection Army' of the Khampas.

> The CIA organized regular airdrops of weapons and supplies to bands of Khampa warriors fighting Chinese occupation in eastern Tibet. India, by then finally aroused to the Chinese threat, joined the effort, directing its foreign intelligence agency, the RAW to cooperate with the CIA in supporting Tibetan resistance efforts. This was one of only a few known instances when the normally adversial CIA and RAW worked together. It was even a rarer example of cooperation, albeit chilly and very limited, between RAW and Pakistani Intelligence; the latter was aiding the US in the effort to supply Tibetan rebels. Bases for Tibetan guerrillas were established in the Indian protectorate of Sikkim and in Nepal, which was equally concerned by the looming Chinese threat.[5]

It was only after Nepal and China signed a secret agreement to defeat the Khampas and the subsequent command of His Majesty the King to the soldiers of the RNA that there was a massive operation resulting in several deaths and the eventure flight of the Khampas. What was most interesting was that the RNA personnel themselves had never seen or known about such sophisticated weapons and communication equipment that they seized from the Khampas. The Chinese remember this episode well, and they don't want to see a similar incident repeat itself.

Another event proved yet again that Nepal is the easiest way

[5] Margolis, op. cit., n. 3 above, p. 90.

in and out of Tibet. The flight of the 17th Karmapa Lama (a 14-year-old boy who occupies one of the most exalted positions in Tibetan Buddhism) via Nepalese territory cheered Tibetan exiles, greatly embarrassed Beijing, and surprised the rest of the world. The flight of the Karmapa Lama and his five followers, including his 24-year-old sister, a Buddhist nun, was a significant development after the Khampa episode of 1974 and the mass movement that took place on the streets of Lhasa in the early 1990s. He is supposed to have used a helicopter, travelled by jeep and train during his gruelling journey to Dharamsala. Nepalese intelligence once again failed to inform the Chinese friends, even as its territory was so significantly exploited for the escape.

In May 2003, a group of Tibetans that some would like to call 'refugees' was handed over to the Chinese authorities by Nepal, generating an international furore and great embarrassment for HMG/N. Some Western governments condemned the Nepalese action.

While these episodes prove that there is international interest in Tibet, which, despite its economic development, still remains one of China's weakest points after Xinjiang, the bordering Nepalese districts of Sindhupalchowk, Dolakha, and Rasua are experiencing a large effect of the insurgency. Moreover, a massive Maoist attack in Dolpa, completely overrunning a police post and looting banks must have stunned the Chinese authorities, as it is a border district with 90 per cent dwellers of the Tibetan-Mongol clan. The Maoists' wish of dividing Nepal in lingual subdivisions would further disturb the Chinese.

Chances of the disturbance spreading deep into Tibet (with an area of 12.284 million sq. km.) cannot be ruled out if Nepal is unable to control the situation, leading to a long and muddled civil war overwhelming the mountainous districts, susceptible as they are to lack of food, shelter, and other basic facilities. Kathmandu has been managing to dispatch food to some of these districts entirely covered with snow during the winter with Chinese help, using their roads passing through Tibet, as they are not connected by roads inside Nepal. Growing disappointment with the Government of Nepal is almost certain, as the adjoining villages on the other side enjoy modern amenities like TVs, VCDs, pool tables, etc. But related as they are with their kith and kin across the border, the Huntington hypothesis invites attention.

> Countries tend to bandwagon with countries of similar culture and to balance against countries with which they lack cultural commonality. This is particularly true with respect to the core states. Their power attracts those who are culturally similar and repels those who are culturally different. For security reasons core states may attempt to incorporate or to dominate some peoples of other civilizations, who, in turn, attempt to resist or to escape such control.[6]

It is interesting that the Maoist Revolutionary Council's draft constitution also proposes to divide their envisaged 'republic' of Nepal into 'nine autonomous regions under a system devised on the basis of self-determination'.

A panel discussion conducted by the Delhi-based Institute of Peace and Conflict Studies (IPCS) for the first time had a series of speakers who disclosed that 'China has its own interests in Nepal, but not to the detriment of India [and] there is evidence that China is aiding the Maoists, and the latter are openly proclaiming their leaning towards Beijing.'[7] Other than this, no reportage or any discussion openly pinpointing Beijing for Nepal's conflict can be found. But in early December 2003, a cache of Chinese pistols on the way to Nepal was found in Khasa. Chinese pistols are used by the Nepal Police, but were also used for the assassination of the chief of armed police Krishna Mohan Shrestha and an Army colonel in the heart of Kathmandu. China would like to distance itself from the current imbroglio, while building on its traditional linkages with the Nepalese.

In December 2001, right after imposition of the state of emergency, Foreign Minister Tang Jiaxuan spoke over the phone with Prime Minister Deuba, making the stand of the Chinese government clear that it would support the Nepalese government in

[6] Huntington, op. cit., n. 2 above, p. 145.

[7] Maj. Gen. Ashok Krishna (retd), Dr Sangeeta Thapaliyal, and Ambassador K.V. Rajan, IPCS Panel Discussion, 7 February 2002: www.ipcs.org

hitting back against the anti-government forces and maintaining peace and stability in Nepal. In April 2002, the Nepalese Foreign Secretary Madhu Raman Acharya paid a visit to China, to inform the Chinese of the internal situation in Nepal. In July 2002, King Gyanendra visited China. President Jiang Zemin, Chairman Li Peng of the NPC, Premier Zhu Rongji, and Vice-President Hu Jintao met him. Leaders of the two countries had high appreciation of friendly cooperation between China and Nepal, and reached an extensive consensus for further cooperation in various fields. During the state visit, President Zemin backed Nepal's fight against the rebels and expressed support for its drive to achieve peace.[8] The king's meeting with Vice-President Hu Jintao was particularly fruitful, as he is known to be the man of China's future. Hu was in charge of Tibet at a very difficult time in its history: Interestingly, this was also the time of Nepal's change to a multiparty democracy.

According to the erstwhile Chinese ambassador to Nepal Wu Congyong, China does not consider the insurgents as Maoists, as they are abusing the name of their great leader.

The *Los Angeles Times* has put Nepal on the world terror map of the US 'as one of the eight countries where the US was planning to send money, materials and military trainers'. In fact, the Americans have pledged a $20 million package which is awaiting Congressional approval, but according to confirmed sources, the assistance package could well go up to $38 million. The American involvement in Nepal adds to Beijing's worries, as the Americans are already in Afghanistan and some Central Asian Republics, apart from their military presence in the Taiwan Straits and the Korean peninsula. Now, a slow encirclement as envisaged by Huntington—though far-fetched—does not seem totally impossible. Perhaps Ambassador Congyong was referring to the growing American involvement in Nepal when he said, 'Nepal should resolve its problems itself.' The stress on the qualifier 'itself' is of special importance.

Summing up, a protracted battle inside Nepalese territory,

[8] CCTV, 21 July 2002.

specially in the mountainous districts adjoining Tibet, impacts China in the following manner:

1. There have been two competing trends in China's future strategic outlook: that of a staunchly nationalistic, relatively insular 'Middle Kingdom'; and that of a great, self-sustained, stable and cooperative country, becoming an economic and military giant of the twenty-first century. Both will require peace and stability in the neighbourhood, which will aid in achieving its goal of rapid economic modernization. Any untoward disturbance in its neighbourhood offsets its concentration from economic development. Hence, the conflict in Nepal is a worry for China's overall political and economic outlook.
2. The complex Sino-US relationship, which has recently been plagued by mutual suspicion, and the continued presence of US troops in the neighbourhood poses multiple quandaries for China. The American troops are currently in the Taiwan Straits, the Korean peninsula, the Central Asian republics, and Afghanistan. American involvement in Nepal in the context of increased violence and human rights violations is a cause of serious concern. Although the Chinese have officially said that they have found no proof that American influence in Nepal is growing, they would want to keep extra vigil in this regard.
3. China would definitely not want the Maoist rebellion to spread into the mountainous districts, specially Manang, Mustang, and Dolpa, with high plateaux and ethnic Tibetan population. Otherwise there will be danger of Nepalese crossing over to Tibet in search of safety and livelihood. It would like to see the situation controlled immediately, specially in Rasua, Ramechap, Dolakha, and Sindhupalchowk having porous borders with the TAR.
4. As tourism in Nepal has been hit hard since the emergency and as Kathmandu is the only foreign capital which has direct air links with Lhasa, China would have to look for alternative arrangements to bring in tourists to Tibet. Additionally, trade between TAR and Nepal, which was witnessing a huge upsurge

till recently, could quickly dwindle, affecting Chinese businesses as border towns become susceptible to violence. Here, its recent decision to open up Nathu La in Sikkim for trade with India deserves attention.

5. As the level of conflict rises with modern weaponry being used both by the RNA and the rebels, these weapons could well sneak into Tibet. A fairly large Tibetan population in Nepal that supports the pro-Tibet movement could use this messy situation inside Nepal to advance their cause.
6. Any foreign role in 'facilitation' or 'mediation' between the government and the rebels could establish the influence foreign powers in Nepal, which could jeopardize the long-standing friendly relations with Nepal.
7. It has been mentioned that India and the US are working in tandem to help Nepal in this hour of grave crisis. Beijing recalls that the last time such a thing happened was during the Khampa revolt. Assistant Secretary of State Rocca has gone further and said that America recognizes India's special relationship with Nepal. China would like to see that the working relationship between the US and India is only to help Nepal help itself, and not at the cost of its over 50 years of influence on Nepal's power centres.
8. There is no dearth of scholars in Nepal who draw parallels between what happened in Sikkim in the 1970s and what is happening in Nepal today. Possible Indian desires to fish in troubled waters will gravely jeopardize Nepal's position as the 'Himalayan wall', thereby threatening China.
9. Since the establishment of diplomatic relations, China has always respected the institution of the monarchy in Nepal and regarded it as a unifying force for all Nepalese. After the establishment of multiparty democracy in 1990, Beijing took some time to reconcile with the changed situation, and, very slowly, began building ties with political parties and leaders in Nepal. The role of the monarchy being reduced further could open a Pandora's box not only for Nepal's future, but for China's long-term interests as well.

10. However, China already has a clear advantage: neither the rebels nor the elite of Kathmandu blame China for the current situation. Although its support to the RNA in logistics and training in comparison to India and the US is less, Beijing is always appreciated for its continuous help to the government. The Maoists too have never criticized China's role in Nepal, even though China does not even regard them as 'Maoists'. It is this advantage that the skilful Chinese diplomats would want to cash in on, specially in the context of the indefinite future course of Nepal and the unknown variables or the new power elite that may emerge in the coming days.

The Chinese central leadership relies on a slow, steady approach to changes around the region, often looking 10 or 20 years down the road. Maintaining the regional status quo promotes external stability, allowing Chinese leaders to control internal stability and issues in their own time. Their diplomacy is famous for its reserve, grandeur, hospitality, and suaveness, which, generally, perplexes the other side as to what they are actually thinking and planning. They have deliberately maintained a distance from the ongoing insurgency and kept a low profile, but have kept an observant eye on the incidents taking place. There is no doubt that China will have high stakes in a chaotic and confused Nepal, but it is also true that Nepalese in general, and its vital institutions in particular, don't have any misgivings about China's intentions, a crucial factor which would probably come to China's advantage, if and when a real crisis occurs.

CHAPTER 11

Future Outlook

A general prediction of Nepal's future vis-à-vis the Maoist movement could be that:

1. the security services will bring an end to the insurgency (as in Punjab); or
2. the Maoists will maintain their base areas, become more aggressive, start encircling the cities, and then take over (as in South Vietnam); or
3. there will finally be a negotiated settlement of the problem (as in the Chittagong Hill Tracts or Mizoram).

But the fourth scenario that virtually no one really considers seriously is what would actually happen if this becomes another never-ending conflict, as in Sri Lanka, Nagaland, or Assam. What if it goes on forever, and, with expenses rising, people get fed up with both sides and not just with the conflict itself? Unwinnable wars go on for years, are far more complex and intractable, and test the patience of the common man and the national economy itself. Sustained conflicts, mostly, have spillover effects on the neighbouring countries as well. Knowing this trend, what will the positions of India and China be once they get the impression that this could go on for years?

At a press conference held by the RNA on 15 August 2002, it was disclosed that more than 3,100 Maoists had died after the imposition of emergency. It was also said that the sympathizers of the rebels could be well over one hundred thousand. But the dent on their arms stockpile was negligible: just over 13 per cent of the weapons that are estimated to be in the possession of the rebels are anticipated to have been captured. According to counter-insurgency experts, it is the recovery of these arms that should be the prime aim. The casualty rate too should be coming down, not going up. A rising casualty rate proves that recruitment is still going on unhindered. The progression from a sympathizer to a *jan* [people's] militia to a hard-core commander is not much. Unless a decisive blow can be delivered at the recruitment stage, the rebels will regroup and re-emerge, even if their best fighters have been wiped out for the time being. But armies all over the democratic world seldom have a say in improving the employment–population ratio, which is what ultimately tends to incite youth (specially of the 15–24 age group) to join an insurgency. This again substantiates the fourth scenario mentioned above.

'Resolving' the Maoist problem has, therefore, several crucial connotations intertwined with it, and does not only mean a military victory. The army could defeat the insurgents, but not the insurgency. For instance, what are the ten thousand-plus cadres going to do after there is a settlement? How are they going to earn their daily living after the battle has, for whatever reason, ended? Resolving the Maoist problem actually involves better management of state affairs, political stability, raising the standard of living of the poor and seriousness on the part of Kathmandu.

The present political anomaly further confuses the situation, and the Nepali state has no other alternative but to: (1) depend fully on the King to manage the situation and bring normalcy back; (2) wait for the constitutional forces to collaborate with one another and then unitedly seek the end of the problem; (3) wait for the Maoists to take over; or (4) wait for foreign intervention to resolve the problem.

Undoubtedly, the political masters were 'shocked' with the King's decision of 4 October 2002, but every sane mind in the country opined that this 'shock therapy' was much needed. However, without the cushion provided by political parties at the centre, it has been a straight battle between the far right and the far left. The political leaders cannot just put the blame on the palace, without putting in their efforts for a national cause and aiming for a prosperous common future for all Nepalese. The Maoists, too, will have to realize that mere killing of soft targets and destroying public and government infrastructure will gradually erode public sympathy that they desperately need.

In the final analysis, therefore, one is left with questions and not answers; mere assumption, not absolute surety; and more uncertainty, not assurance, regarding the future of Nepal and the likely course of the Maoist movement.

1. Leaders of political parties have been calling for an all-party government, restoration of the Parliament, and, eventually, elections to the lower house. Will mere elections and formation of governments resolve the woes of the people?
2. The Maoists have been demanding elections for a Constituent Assembly. Will this resolve the problem, or will it further disorganize the state? Will they be held under the shadow of guns, or without it? Will the assembly of multiple arrays of elected representatives from a diverse array of parties agree on a single draft of the new constitution? What if the new constitution fragments the country into numerous states, or divides it in the pre-unification phase? Or, more importantly, what if the new constitution too soon meets the same fate as that of its predecessor?
3. There have been quite a few takers for the demand of making Nepal a secular state. Will it end the present discrimination against the minority scheduled castes and dalits in the country, or initiate, for the first time, a religious war by antagonizing the majority Hindus? Will Hinduism cease to become the state religion, or will it in turn be used by fanatics for political gains, just as in India?
4. It has been demanded that the RNA be put under Parliament's control. Will it correct the constitutional dichotomy regarding its use and place the prime minister as a *de facto* controller of the force, or upset the army's chain of command, thereby putting national security in a further shambles?

Hence, what can possibly work and perhaps answer the above questions is only by emphasizing the points of convergence between the monarchy, political parties, and the Maoists, and setting aside differences for the sake of achieving the common cause of saving Nepal from mayhem and ultimate destruction. Political experiments for short-term gains and factional rivalry will, as we have seen in the past, result in disappointment and turmoil for an even longer period. All the three powers will, in the end, have to comprehend that Nepal, the birthplace of Lord Gautam Buddha and at one time a zone of peace, cannot be allowed to sink to the status of a 'failed state' by not managing itself, correcting its own follies, and achieving its aspirations.

ANNEXURE I

The 40-Point List of Demands Submitted by Baburam Bhattarai to the then Prime Minister Sher Bahadur Deuba on 4 February 1996[1]

DEMANDS RELATED TO NATIONALISM

1. All unequal treaties including the 1950 Treaty of Peace and Friendship with India ought to be abolished.
2. The Integrated Mahakali Treaty reached with India should be abolished, as it is anti-national and detrimental to the long-term interests of the country.
3. The Indo-Nepal open border must be regulated and vehicles with Indian number plates should not be allowed to enter Nepalese territory.
4. Gorkha recruitment camps must be closed down and Nepalese must be guaranteed respectable employment inside the country itself.
5. Nepalese themselves should be encouraged to take up occupations inside the country and a work permit system should be announced before allowing foreign workers to work in Nepal.
6. Dominance of foreign investment and their monopolist capital in financial institutions, industries and other businesses must be stopped.
7. [The] Customs policy should be framed in order to [for] best developing a self-reliant national economy.
8. Imperialist and expansionist cultural pollution and molestation must be curtailed. The import and distribution of vulgar Indian cinema, videos and publications must be immediately stopped.
9. Imperialist, expansionist penetration inside the country in the name of INGOs and NGOs must be stopped.

[1] Translated by the author

DEMANDS RELATED TO THE PUBLIC AND ITS WELL-BEING

10. A new constitution must be drafted by the people's representatives elected in order to establish a people's republican state.
11. All special rights and privileges of the King and the royal family should be abolished.
12. The army, police and the administration must be totally controlled by the people.
13. All oppressive regulations including the Security Act should be abolished.
14. Political prisoners arrested in Rukum, Rolpa, Jajarkot, Gorkha, Kavre, Sindhupalchowk, Sindhuli, Dhalusa, Ramechap and other districts ought to be released.
15. Armed police operations going on in various districts must be stopped.
16. [The] Whereabouts of Dilip Chaudhary, Bhuwan Thapa Magar, Prabhakar Subedi who have been missing from police custody must be disclosed and the culprits should be brought to justice.
17. People killed during the people's movement of 1990 must be declared martyrs, their families should receive compensation and the culprits must be hardheartedly [*sic*] punished.
18. Nepal must be declared a secular state.
19. Girls should be given equal property rights to those of their brothers.
20. State oppression of the people of the lower castes must be stopped. Areas that have dominance of the people of the scheduled castes and tribes must be given autonomy.
21. Discrepancy against the scheduled castes and tribes must be stopped and untouchability ought to be fully banned.
22. People of all languages must be given opportunities by the state. Education in the mother tongue must be allowed till the primary level.
23. Freedom of expression and publishing must be fully guaranteed. Government media must be given autonomy.
24. Academic liberty of intellectuals, poets, artists must be guaranteed.
25. Sectoral dissimilarity between the Terai and the hills must be brought down and there must be a proper balance maintained between the villages and the cities.
26. Local-bodies must be given full powers and adequate resources.

DEMANDS RELATED TO PEOPLE'S LIVING

27. Land should be of the tillers. Lands of rich landlords must be confiscated and distributed to the landless.
28. Property of commission agents and the bourgeois capitalists must be confiscated and nationalized. Capital stuck up in unproductive sectors must be put to use for industrialization.
29. All must be guaranteed of employment and 'unemployed allowance' must be given to those that are jobless.
30. Minimum wage of workers and labourers working in industrial and agricultural sectors must be set by the state and strictly reinforced.
31. Landless people must be arranged (*sic*) with adequate living conditions.
32. Bank loans taken by poor peasants must be written off. Small time entrepreneurs ought to be encouraged with adequate credit to finance their businesses.
33. Fertilizers and plant seeds must be cheap and easily available. The produce of peasants must get [a] good price and access to the market.
34. Flood and drought victims must be rehabilitated by the state.
35. The people must be guaranteed with free and modern health services. Commercialization of the education sector must stop.
36. Price rise must stop and the supply of daily essential commodities must be unobstructed. Daily wage must be set in proportion to the price rise.
37. Supply of drinking water, roads and electricity must be taken to all the villages of the country.
38. State must protect and encourage the small cottage industries.
39. Corruption, black-marketing, smuggling and commission taking must be strictly curtailed.
40. State must look after the disabled, orphans, the elderly and the children.

ANNEXURE II

Fundamental Laws of Guerrilla Warfare

It is an interesting fact worth noting that, subsequent to their decision to opt for an armed struggle, the Maoists adopted a strategy of guerrilla warfare that is not very different from the styles of warfare that we have seen in China, Malaya, the Philippines, Peru, South Vietnam, and other places. In fact, the stratagem of warfare delicately framed and put to action successfully by Mao Tse-tung has definitely been their most fervently-held belief. There are other volumes of guerrilla warfare strategy designed by veterans of the communist revolutionary world, namely Gen. Vo Nguyen Giap, Che Guevara, Comrade Gonzalo, etc.

This author selected some of their most significant directives and commandments of guerrilla warfare, as they bear a good semblance to the approach taken by the Maoists years and even decades after they were first put to use.[1]

1. A small striking force can maintain itself against a superior enemy only with the help of guerrilla warfare.
2. Know your enemy and know yourself, and you can fight hundred battles without disaster.
3. In time of war, you have to take your lead from the enemy. When your enemy changes his strategy or tactics, you have to do the same. In every war, a strategy is always made up of a number of tactics that are considered to be of great strategic importance, so you have to try to smash those tactics.
4. In most cases, the revolutionaries will have to start from nothing.

[1] Based on Sun Tzu, *The Art of War*, Harrisburg, Pennsylvania: Military Service Publishing, 1944, p. 167; Gen. Vo Nguyen Giap, *People's War, People's Army*, Hanoi: Foreign Languages Publishing, 1961, p. 87; Mao Tse Tung, *Problems of China's Revolutionary War*, vol. I, *Selected Works*, p. 53; *On the Protracted War*, vol. II, *Selected Works*, p. 4; *The Struggle in the Chingkiang Mountains*, vol. II, *Selected Works*, New York: International Publishers; Che Guevara, *Guerrilla Warfare*: www.che.lives.com

Secretly, they will have to organize, first, cells, and then extensive wings of organization. Around the cells, they must build political propaganda groups to win popular support, and teams of revolutionaries to intimidate where propaganda fails. Demonstrations, strikes, interruption by frontal sister organizations must be a standard phenomenon.

5. Insurgents have to establish themselves in the countryside in isolated, difficult terrain where the governing authorities are the weakest. They should silently take control of isolated villages where they form guerrilla bases, operate a parallel administration and legal hierarchies, collecting taxes, policing, administering justice, recruiting, and so forth.
6. In Phase I, revolutionary forces should conduct guerrilla and terrorist operations to control as much of the population as possible. In Phase II, guerrilla forces should consolidate into regular units to attack isolated government outposts. In the climactic Phase III, large units should be formed to establish full military control over an area, allowing and encouraging the civilian population to rise up in support of the revolution.
7. A practical breakdown of the government's rural administration is required. Then the area becomes the 'commissariat' and the 'popular base'.
8. Guerrillas must be to the population as little fishes in water. The population not only provides the guerrillas with water, food, and intelligence, but also gives them perfect cover and concealment. They may be peasants in the afternoon and guerrillas at night.
9. A revolutionary armed struggle in any country has common fundamental laws. A revolutionary armed struggle in each country has characteristics and laws of its own too.
10. It is necessary to bring about a brief reign of terror in every rural area, otherwise one could never suppress the activities of the counter-revolutionaries in the countryside or overthrow the authority of the gentry. Terror is, therefore, a psychological weapon of unbelievable power.
11. *Organization*, *Terrorism*, *Guerrilla Warfare*, and *Mobile Warfare* are the basic phases of revolutionary war strategy.[2] At the same time, five

[2] Mao developed a two-stage strategy, which started with guerrilla warfare, and slowly progressed through mobile warfare to victory.

other strategic principles of revolutionary warfare have been identified.

(a) Preserving oneself and annihilating the enemy.
(b) Establishing strategic bases.
(c) Mobilizing the masses.
(d) Seeking outside support.
(e) Unifying the effort.

12. Avoid superior forces. But if guerrillas meet superior forces, they should withdraw when the enemy advances; they should harass them when they settle down; they should attack them when they are exhausted; they should chase when they flee.
13. Surprise is the main element of successful guerrilla tactics.
14. Attacks must be carefully planned. Guerrillas should always attack on their own initiative.
15. Guerrillas should concentrate on weaker enemy forces.[3] Guerrillas should deliver a violent, lightning blow and seek a lightning decision.
16. If conditions are unfavourable, the guerrillas should disperse and shift immediately.
17. All prevalent political conditions and local seeds of conflict must be exploited to the advantage of the revolution. Sabotage, armed struggles, and operations must be conducted in rural areas, while cities must be used for propaganda.
18. It is not necessary to wait until all conditions for making revolution exist: the insurrection can create them.
19. A guerrilla fighter needs to have a good knowledge of the surrounding countryside, the paths of entry and escape, the possibilities of speedy manoeuvre, good hiding places; naturally, also, he must count on the support of the people.
20. No battle, skirmish, or combat should be fought without the possibility of winning.
21. Hit and run, wait, lie in ambush, again hit and run, and thus, repeatedly, without giving any rest to the enemy.
22. The arms of the enemy, his ammunition, and his habits must be considered, because the principal source of provision for the guer-

[3] Peng Teh-huai elaborated this rule in an interview with Edgar Snow in *Red Star Over China*. 'In a regular engagement with enemy troops the partisans must exceed the enemy in numbers. But if the enemy's regular troops are moving, resting, or poorly guarded, a swift, determined surprise flank attack on an originally vital spot or the enemy's line can be made by a much smaller group.'

rilla force is precisely in enemy armaments. If there is a choice, the preference should be of the same type as that used by the enemy, since the greatest problem of the guerrilla band is lack of ammunition, which the opponent must provide.

23. The popular work should first be aimed at securing secrecy. That is, each peasant, each member of the society in which action is taking place, should be asked not to mention what he sees and hears. Later, help should be sought from inhabitants whose loyalty to the revolution offers greater guarantees. After that, use should be made of these persons in missions of contact, for transporting goods or arms, as guides in the zones familiar to them. Still later, it is possible to arrive at organized mass action at the centres of work, of which the final result will be the general strike.
24. Faced with counteraction by the police, the revolutionaries will be hardened, solidified, and experienced.
25. When the guerrilla band has reached a respectable power in arms and number of combatants, it ought to proceed to the formation of new columns. This is an act similar to that in a beehive, when, at a given moment it releases a new queen, which goes to another region with a part of the swarm. The mother hive with the most notable guerrilla chief will stay in the less dangerous places, while the new columns will penetrate other enemy territories.
26. As the circumstances of the war require, the guerrilla band can dedicate itself exclusively to fleeing from an encirclement which is the enemy's only way of forcing the band into a decisive fight that could be unfavourable; it can also change the battle into a counter-encirclement (small bands of men are presumably surrounded by the enemy, when suddenly the enemy himself is surrounded by stronger contingents; or men located in a safe place serve as a lure, leading to the encirclement and annihilation of the entire troops and supply of an attacking force).
27. Movement at night is an important characteristic of the guerrilla band, enabling it to advance into position for an attack, and, where the danger of betrayal exists, to mobilize in new territory. The numerical inferiority of the band necessitates that attacks always be carried out by surprise.
28. In any combat between a regular force and a guerrilla band, it is always possible to know one from the other by their different manner of fire: a great amount of firing on the part of the regular army; sporadic and accurate shots on the part of the guerrillas.

TABLE A2.1: *JANJATI* POPULATION OF NEPAL

Caste/Linguistic Group	District/Area
Kami, Sarki, Damai, Gaine, Badi	Wherever the population of Brahmin/ Chhetri rises, primarily in the mid-hills, and Badis in the western hills.
Newars[1]	Kathmandu, Lalitpur, Bhaktapur, and other business hubs.
Magar	Between the Kali Gandaki River to the Bheri River in the west, and sporadically in the mid-hills.
Gurung	Between the Kali Gandaki Modi River to the hills east of Budi Gandaki, and in Annapurna, and Machapuchre, along with the mid-Terai.
Tamang	The mid-hills between Budhigandaki and Likhu Khola, Sunkoshi River in the east, except in Kathmandu valley.
Khumbu-Rai	Between Liku Khola Sunkoshi to Arun River in the east. Patchy settlements in the Terai as well.
Limbu	The hill area between Arun River to Mechi River in the east, and sporadic settlements in the Terai.
Lepcha	Taplejung district.
Sherpa	Solukhumbu.
Sunuwar	North-east Likukhola of Ramechap district.
Jirel	Jiri area of Dolakha district.
Surel	Surikhola area of Dolakha district.
Thami	Tamakoshi Siran area of Dolakha.
Pahari	South-east area of Kavre district.
Chepang	Dhading, Makawanpur, Gorkha, and Chitawan districts.
Dura	Dura hills of Lamjung district.
Tharu	Dang, Bardia, Kailali, and Kanchanpur.[2]

[1] Note that some population experts do not consider Newars as *janjatis*.

[2] Dev Gurung, 'The Question of Nationalism in Nepal: A Study', *Disabodh*, nos. 3–4, January–June 1999.

Bibliography

Arpi, Caude, *The Fate of Tibet: When Big Insects Eat Small Insects*, New Delhi: Har-Anand Publications, 1999.

Bhasin, Avtar Singh, ed., *Nepal's Relations with India and China*, New Delhi: SIBA EXIM Publishers, vol. I, 1994.

Bhattarai, Babu Ram, 'The Birth of a Republic': www.humanrights.de-n-nepal-politics

Bhatty, Maqbool Ahmad, *Great Powers and South Asia: Post Cold War Trends*, Islamabad: Institute of Regional Studies, 1996.

Chari, P. R, Suba Chandran, and Mallika Joseph, *Terrorism and its Repercussions on International Politics*, New Delhi: Friedrich-Ebert-Stiftung (India), and Institute of Peace and Conflict Studies, 2003.

Dahal, Dev Raj, *The Challenge of Good Governance: Decentralization and Development in Nepal*, Kathmandu: Centre for Governance and Development Studies, 1996.

Diamond, Louise and John McDonald, *Multi-Track Diplomacy: A Systems Approach to Peace*, Connecticut: Kumarian Press, 1996.

Dixon, Aubrey C. and Otto Heilbrunn, *Communist Guerrilla Warfare*, New York: Friedrich A. Praeger Publishers, 1962.

Dutt, V.K., *India's Foreign Policy in a Changing World*, New Delhi: Vikas Publications, 1999.

Gautam, Pushkar, 'Borderline War', *Nepali Times*, 1–7 March 2002.

Giap, vo Nguyen, *People's War, People's Army*, Hanoi: Foreign Languages Publishing House, 1961.

Guevara, Che, *Guerilla Warfare*: www.che.lives.com

HMG Nepal, *Constitution of the Kingdom of Nepal 2047 B.C.*, Kathmandu: HMG, 2047 B.S., 1991.

Huntington, Samuel P., *The Clash of Civilizations and the Remaking of the World Order*, New York: First Touchestone, 1997, p. 315.

Institute of Strategic Studies, *Strategic Studies*, vol. XXII, no. 3, Islamabad, 2002.

International Development Research Centre, *The Responsibility to Protect: Report on the International Commission on Intervention and State Sovereignty*, Ottawa, 2001.

Jentleson, Bruce W. and Thomas G. Paterson, *Encyclopedia of US Foreign Relations*, New York: Oxford University Press, vols. 1–4, 1997.

Joseph, Mallika, 'Security Threat Assessment of Naxalites in India', 2001: www.ipcs.org

Josse, M. R., 'Riddle in a Mystery inside an Enigma', *The Kathmandu Post*, 10 January 2001.

Kaplan, Robert D., *The Coming Anarchy*, New York: Vintage Books, 2000.

Khanal, Krishna P., 'Party Politics and Governance: The Role of Leadership', in *State, Leadership and Politics in Nepal*, ed. Dhruba Kumar, Kathmandu: Centre for Nepal and Asian Studies, 1995.

Khatri, Sridhar K., 'Nepal in the International System: The Limits of Power of a Small State', in *The Political Economy of Small States*, ed. Anand Aditya, Kathmandu: Nepal Foundation for Advanced Studies, and FES (Nepal), 1998.

Kumar, Dhruba, *Domestic Conflict and Crisis of Governability in Nepal*, Kathmandu: Centre for Nepal and Asian Studies, 2000.

Lama, Mahendra P., 'India Should not Interfere in Nepal', *Nepali Times*, 16–30 December 2002.

Lohani, Mohan Prasad., Preface, *Nepal-Bharat Khula Simana Sakaratmak tatha Nakaratma Pakchya Haru* ('Indo-Nepal Open Border: Positive and Negative Aspects), Kathmandu: IFA/FES (Nepal), 2002.

Margolis, Eric S., *War at the Top of the World*, New Delhi: Roli Books, 2001.

Mathew, Joseph C., *Ethnic Conflict in Bhutan*, New Delhi: Nirala Publications, 1999.

McCuen, John J., *The Art of Counter-Revolutionary War*, London: Faber and Faber, 1966.

Muni, S. D., *India and Nepal: A Changing Relationship*, New Delhi: Konark Publishers, 1996.

Muni, S. D. and Lok Raj Baral, *Refugees and Regional Security in South Asia*, Colombo: Regional Centre for Strategic Studies, 1996.

Pokhrel, Shankar, *Maobadi Ugrabampanth ra Prajatantrik Nikas* (Maoist Extremism and a Democratic Resolution), Kathmandu: Ekkaisaun Satabdi Publishers, 2001.

Prachanda, *Document of the Second National Conference of the Communist Party of Nepal (Maoist)*, 2001.

Pushpalal, *Brief History of Nepal's Communist Movement*, Kathmandu: Pushpalal Memorial Academy, 2000.

Thompson, Robert, *Defeating Communist Insurgency*, New York: Friedrich A. Praeger Publishers, 1966.

Toffler, Alvin, *The Third Wave*, New York: Bantam Books, 1991.

Tung, Mao Tse, *Problems of China's Revolutionary War*, vol. I, New York: New York International Publishers, 1954.

Tzu, Sun, *The Art of War*, Harrisburg, Pennsylvania: Military Service Publishing, 1944.

Uprety, Hari and Ananda P. Srestha, *Conflict Resolution and Governance in Nepal*, Kathmandu: NEFAS, and FES (Nepal), 2003.

Wen, Qi, *China: A General Survey*, Beijing: Foreign Languages Press, 1984.

Yew, Lee Kuan, *From Third World to First: The Singapore Story*, New York: Harper Collins Publishers, 1999.

RCSS PUBLICATIONS

- *Defence, Technology and Cooperative Security in South Asia: Report on the Proceedings of the Tenth Summer Workshop* (RCSS, 2004)
- *Environment Development and Human Security: Perspectives from South Asia* (2003)
- *Terrorism in South Asia: Impact on Development and Democratic Process* (SIPRA, 2003)
- *South Asia and the War on Terrorism* (India Research Press, 2003)
- *Shaping the Future–A South Asian Civil Society Dialogue* (RCSS, July 2002)
- *Small Arms and Human Insecurity* (RCSS, July 2002)
- *SAARC in the Twenty-First Century: Towards a Cooperative Future* (July 2002)
- *Memories of a Genocidal Partition: The Haunting Tale of Victims, Witnesses and Perpetrators* (RCSS, July 2002)
- *South Asian Security Futures: A Dialogue of Director's Regional Strategic Studies Institutes* (March 2002)
- *Security and Governance in South Asia* (September 2001)
- *Globalization and Non-Traditional Security in South Asia* (September 2001)
- *Security in the New Millennium* (India Research Press, 2001)
- *The Simla Agreement 1972: Its Wasted Promise* (Manohar, 2001)

RCSS Newsletter

A quarterly bulletin, it publishes a brief report of RCSS activities, presentations at its workshops on topics of contemporary interest and news and programmes of the RCSS and its alumnae.

RCSS Policy Studies

34 Indo-Pak Conflicts: Ripe to Resolve? (Manohar, 2005)
33 Small Arms and the Security Debate in South Asia (Manohar, 2005)
32 New Nuclear Triangle and China's Role in South Asia (forthcoming)
31 Stability through Economic Cooperation in a Nuclear Environment (Manohar, 2005)
30 Multi-Track Diplomacy between India and Pakistan: A Conceptual Framework for Sustainable Security (Manohar, 2005)
29 The Role of Mediation in Resolving India-Pakistan Conflict: Parameters and Possibilities (Manohar, 2005)
28 HIV/AIDS as a Security Threat to India (Manohar, 2005)
27 Nepal's Maoist Movement and Implications for India and China (Manohar, 2005)
26 Elite Perceptions in Foreign Policy: Role of Print Media in Influencing India-Pakistan Relations, 1989–1999 (Manohar, 2004)
25 Nuclar Risk Reduction Measures and Restraint Regime in South Asia (Manohar, 2004)
24 River Water Sharing Problem Between India and Pakistan: Case Study of the Indus Basin Water Treaty (June 2004)
23 Christianity and Political Conflict in India: The Case of Gujarat (June 2002)

Fellowship in South Asian Alternatives (FISAA) Monograph

- Water, Power And People: A South Asian Manifesto on the Politics and Knowledge of Water (1997)
- The Nuclear Debate: Ironies and Immoralities (1998)

Others

- *Directory of Individuals and Institutions Engaged in South Asian Strategic Studies* (1998).